THE BEST
AUSTRALIAN
POEMS
2010

THE BEST
AUSTRALIAN
POEMS
2010

Edited by

ROBERT ADAMSON

Published by Black Inc.,
an imprint of Schwartz Media Pty Ltd
37–39 Langridge Street
Collingwood VIC 3066 Australia
email: enquiries@blackincbooks.com
http://www.blackincbooks.com

ISBN 9781863954969

Printed in Australia by Griffin Press

Contents

Introduction

The subject? At the heart of the various influences, concerns and interests
addressed here lies, quite obviously, the problematic of the lyric voice in
turbulent times. The lyric: at once a singular voice and a multi-voiced
part-song, replete with echoes; at moments, of necessity, anti-lyrical in
the extreme. What?—MICHAEL PALMER, Active Boundaries

The Best Australian Poems 2010 vibrates with 'correspondences'. The images that appear in some poems seem to be reflected in others, and certain themes weave their way along the lines until the individual poems begin to read like stanzas in some epic story of the history of this country. It may be a fragmented narrative, but a great thing about poetry is its ability to zoom in on some tiny detail to magnify and reveal its significance. So poets can recreate a moment of time, or listen to the trees speak, as Baudelaire did in his poem '*Correspondances*'; his 'forest of symbols' is now a forest of broadcasting towers, still emitting confusing messages, and poetry is one way to decipher lyrics from electronic jargon.

When selecting these poems I was surprised by how many poets wrote about similar subjects. Reading for *The Best Australian Poems 2010*, I put aside more than seven poems that mentioned bats; five of these actually had 'bats' in their titles. Last year I said it was the year of women poets. There were plenty of bird poems as well and not all of them were about birds. Is this the year of the bat? Don't let it put you off; I ended up only selecting three of the bat poems and each one of them is a stunning work of art.

Makes one wonder, what caused this sudden slew of poems about bats? There have been birds in our poems since Charles

Harpur's flight of ducks escaped on a 'thousand wings' from the sound of some 'Fowler's gun'. Now flying foxes and tiny horse-shoe bats seem to be the *de rigueur* subject for lyric poetry. It's true both Les Murray and Judith Beveridge have written very fine poems about bats, but there was a decent interlude between them. I considered including some of the other bat poems but I didn't want to weaken the impact of the three I'd already accepted by Martin Harrison, Debbie Lim and Andrew Slattery. Remember in China bats are seen as auspicious animals and are welcomed as signs of happiness and luck! One last bat-thought: recently scientists discovered that flying foxes are one of the important pollinators of our eucalyptus forests, doing more good than harm when they eat Morton Bay figs, other fruits and the nectar from wattles.

I put aside this coincidence of bats. I decided to look for poems that worked as poems on their own terms. Robert Creeley once said that 'poetry is not made of ideas but words' and this is a good tip; if you look at the way a poem is put together, you'll probably discover what the poem is saying becomes a lot clearer. It's an old pitfall to gather poems on a particular subject or theme. It's even tricky to collect an anthology containing only sonnets; it's been done, but rarely successfully.

I've always noted Creeley's advice that you discover what a poem's about during the process of writing it, that poetry is a way to make something rather than represent it. 'Form is never more than an extension of content' is a line Charles Olson wrote to describe the poetry of process, poetry of the open field. However, this line makes more sense when you read the corollary Creeley added: 'Content is never more than an extension of form.' Poetry is never simply *about* something; a poem is a made thing, some-thing that didn't exist before.

The poems in this anthology have been selected from work written or published over the last twelve months, up until August this year. I'm sure there were fine poems that I missed or somehow slipped by. There are so many people writing poetry in Australia, hundreds of seriously persistent poets –

to the ones who missed out, all I can say is I'm sorry and to just keep writing. I wanted this issue to be different from last year's; quite a few poets have said to me that these anthologies seem the same. I assure you this one is different. There are 108 poets published here; of these, 49 are poets that weren't included in the previous year's edition. Some poets don't publish or even write poems every year, and there *are* many reasons not to publish.

When I was younger, I found lasting inspiration in a few lines Robert Duncan published in his statement of poetics in *The New American Poetry*: 'Poetry is the very life of the soul: the body's discovery that it can dream. And perish into its own imagination. Why should one's art then be an achievement? Why not, more, an adventure?' At the time this was an unfashionable point of view (it still is): it was the 1970s, the days when foundations for 'creative writing schools' were being built, and the careers in poetry were not far behind. The following sentences, though I didn't heed them, were the ones I found most reassuring: 'We dreamed not originally of publishing. What a paltry concern. No child of the imagination would center there. But we dreamed of song and the reality of romance.' I think this applies to the poets who have published more than two books. Also, it's worth the wait; a first book should never be rushed into publication.

This anthology will bear many readings. The poems are in layers rather than clusters; you will notice the alphabetical shuffle of the index has scattered poems throughout the book like a kaleidoscope. This seemingly random placement has created an abstracting effect that's more interesting than any ordering into groups based on content or form. The reader will notice straight off by flicking through the pages that I have published several long poems. This is a way of showing an extended example of a poet's work; there are poets who need space to perform at their best. The beautiful and strange poem 'Sanssouci' by Robert Gray demonstrates his lapidary ability with imagery. There's no question that Gray is a poet working at full power here. There's Ken

Bolton, Pam Brown and Joanne Burns, who write with a charm that makes reading them a joy. Beware, the ground is full of hidden wombat holes and any slip means death – these three use irony and wit to undercut any emotion that might lapse into sentimentality. Their poems are columns of breath, foundations of the anthology in some ways, especially when coupled with the extraordinary poems by Astrid Lorange and Adam Formosa, both younger poets coming into their own. There are also new poems by Chris Edwards and Michael Farrell. When Peter Porter back in 2005 called Edwards and Farrell 'two agents of a dispersing avant-garde', he didn't predict, in the tide created by the dispersing innovators, that a momentum might build and carry them onward. Here they are with two very strong new poems. 'Guileless' by Chris Edwards is a sign of real staying power; this poem is alive with the energy of making.

Then come what I might call new confessionals with a twist, David Brooks and Geoffrey Lehmann. Both poets, in these works, 'spill the beans' as they say. It must have taken some courage to write poems like these. Well, at least to have allowed them to be published in such a public way. The twist will become apparent when you read and compare these very different approaches to biographical poetry.

The reason I have published two poems by some poets is simple: I couldn't print enough to prove how good their work is at the moment. Rhyll McMaster is a poet I have followed since her first book; she is one of our most original poets, and the poems she sent in this year are probably her best. Then there are two wonderful, prayer-like poems from Anne Elvey, who writes lucidly about the mystery of the soul. Sarah Holland-Batt is just getting better all the time and two poems tell of her growing power. Speaking of power, three new poems from Judith Beveridge demonstrate why her reputation is so high these days: the lines and enjambments are charged with an exquisite grace and intensity, and these poems also have a gentleness at their core, which is her great strength. Then come the Zen masters of the craft, Jennifer Maiden and Gig Ryan, both with great new poems that enrich and deepen this anthology. Claire Potter and Susan Fealy are relatively new poets. Potter's first book, *Swallow*, is a stunner; it was released in October this year. Both poets were published by *Meanjin* (along with many others in this anthology). So let me say, here's to *Meanjin* for such acumen! Also thanks to the newspapers and journals that keep poetry before the public; the *Age*'s *A2*, the *Sydney Morning Herald* and the *Australian* have circulations of up to 400,000, and *Australian Book Review, HEAT, Blast, Island, Overland, Southerly, Westerly, Blue Dog, Quadrant* and on-line journals like *Jacket* and *Cordite* are vital in lasting ways and crucial to the development of our poetry. Here I must thank Black Inc. for *The Best Australian Poems*; its annual contribution to our culture is rare and profound.

Some poems will drift free from any mooring and float out over their own waters; they don't fit categories, and a few of these came up this year. The 'goat' poems by Anthony Lawrence and John Kinsella can be read as examples. Another outbreak of coincidence, Carl Jung's favourite quote on this (he called it 'synchronicity') was from Lewis Carroll's *Through the Looking Glass* in which the White Queen says to Alice: 'It's a poor sort of memory that only works backwards.' I don't know what these two archrivals will make of it when they see their 'goat' poems published alongside each other. Anthony Lawrence has another poem, a searing piece about a rift in a relationship, possibly a dialogue between body and soul, the psychological inscape of a decision: 'knowing you'd find such self-discipline irresistible'. Above all, it's a fine poem about a person surviving a period when 'light and dark had not become epiphanies'.

Another trace or thread that runs through the book is an interest in both ancient and contemporary China. Several poems touch on this connection. Barry Hill has a fine poem, 'Plum Juice'; it is spare and melancholy in tone, and refers to Tu Fu, the great poet of the Tang Dynasty. There is also Hill's 'Gannets' – it's chilling to read these lines as his words *become* the birds, plummeting into a froth of red seawater and schools of mackerel, homicidal penitents. It's a stunning performance.

Michelle Leber has written about the discovery of silk by Lei Zu, who was the wife of the Yellow Emperor (2697–2595 BC). Leber's imaginative reach back through time is impressive. There's another poem set in the China of 1925 by Eileen Chong, who writes about the love affair between Lu Xun and Xu Guang-ping: 'spare a thought for those scrambling to find a way out of this nest of scorpions.'

There is a tightly written poem about Charles Darwin's eight-year study of barnacles that chimes with L.K. Holt's clean-lined and witty 'Darwin's Taxidermist'. These in turn correspond in history with 'Alfred Wallace's Dragon' by A. Frances Johnson. Another poem from this cluster is Meredith Wattison's 'The Naming of the Devil', a clever, flexible poem about marsupials in Tasmania. Some poets trace a sense of place along with art history, such as Kate Middleton's light-filled 'Condor's Dandenongs' and Lisa Gorton's poem with my favourite title, 'The Humanity of Abstract Painting'.

There's a fine poem by Chloe Wilson in response to a Joy Hester painting. Jenni Nixon's 'Cockatoo Island' reaches back to the 1800s. She mentions Captain Thunderbolt the Bushranger and his Indigenous wife, Mary Ann Budd. There's the unclassifi-able poem 'Mortal to Immortal' by Lionel Fogarty, where 'The morning spits up the sun', and Ali Cobby Eckermann has written delicate 'Yankunytjatjara Love Poems' set in 'a field of zebra finch Dreaming' at a time 'when the soft blanket of language hums'.

Astrid Lorange's ingenious 'Attraction' plunges us back into a contemporary zone, a sleek poem shaped by wit and humour. There are political poems, without being too didactic – on cli-mate change and watching war on TV, and on political refugees who flee the horror of the wars our country has involved us in. There are satirical poems and personal lyrics, while others tell a story like Allison Browning's 'Fuel', where a young couple buys petrol at a stark service station. They are a bit like a couple that has strayed from a Raymond Carver story, except this poem is from a woman's point of view. And there's whimsy; we even have a '3D Homer Simpson' by Nathan Curnow, a cardboard cut-out who, as the poem develops, becomes the narrator explaining himself.

In other poems we have literary references bouncing back and forth: Laurie Duggan's 'The Exeter Book', Jen Jewel Brown's 'Mary Shelley's Man'. There's a 'Dear John Letter' by Meera Atkinson, influenced by the writings of two Hungarian-French analysts and theorists! I think many of the best poems 'tell all the truth' – *and tell it slant* – drawn from so-called life experiences. I looked for tough poems that didn't pull their punches and more or less came straight out with it. I was thrilled to find Adam Formosa's 'The Sparrow', based on alternative culture, among other things, and set mainly on the streets. Formosa could become the Thom Gunn of Wollongong for a while, before travelling on to better things: his first book of poetry. As Emily Dickinson reminds us,

Truth must dazzle gradually
Or every man be blind—

Two major Australian poets died in the last year, Peter Porter and Randolph Stow. They were both important innovators of contemporary poetry in their different ways. Porter was a more public figure than Stow, who was inward looking and quite a dark lyric poet. Porter could be lyrical too, but was more an Augustan poet of culture and satire. Porter was, because of his radio and TV appearances, a palpable presence who was a part of our ongoing conversation. Stow became a reclusive figure over recent decades. However, this didn't weaken his poetry's force; in fact, the more silent Stow became, the more I read *A Counterfeit Silence* (his selected poems). It sits on my desk right now as I write these words. His fierce imagination will always exist for me in that place beyond the pale, 'In the wrack of the crow. In a desert of broken quartz.' I accepted a poem for this book by Craig Sherborne that's dedicated to Peter Porter. It's called 'The Great God Gatsby' and engages with Porter's last book, *Better Than God*. So now these two important people have gone from the world as our friends and companions; however they have both left us the precious cargo of their books.

Robert Adamson

Thanks to Michael Palmer for permission to quote from the preface of his book, Active Boundaries *(New Directions, 2008).*

Language(s)

for John Mateer

I'll speak you mine, you speak me yours
since all's in the telling, content, form

to mangle the Master's eavesdropping
on subalterns' whispers, going Chinese

subversive, maybe just incomprehensible
or incomprehensibly blunt. My Farsi

the fierce Real or the sad Other of the Master-
Signifiers, Sylvester to their Tweety or

a Roadrunner, mercurial, radical
to thwart the tyrant's order of things? I'll say

something to you, you say something
to me, and bar me from understanding

this or that – who'd ever want me
in control, so damn crazy to accumulate

secrets, gossip, sedition, gesticulation
even if I am, say, sentient, so what

's in it for you? Forge a discourse
to chain your/my tongue/s. You'll write me

yours, I write you mine, and we'll relish
the mystery of the written sign, the tricky

similitude between things, incoherent
thorn in the monoglot Master's eye.

Ali Alizadeh

By Accident

Tonight I can write if not the saddest lines,
the sort that drive a resonant ache in deep
like the shockingly slow cover of 'Fast Car'
I heard as I lay in a black hotel room
feeling fine, then lines that gather drabber kinds
of sadness, like knowing which were the best days:
sad like a stand-up routine that's not working,
or the dated cover art on videos;
sad by accident like the fall of a song
from edgy to catchy to muzak classic,
or was that a fatality like fresh clerks
finding out the translucent brutalities
and slender consolations of office life?

Tonight I can write for example: the stars
are shot-holes in the roof of a ghost town hall,
and schoolie debris is strewn on cold beach sand:
the vomit of losers, a solitary thong,
sad like someone who has heard by accident
a snatch of what people say behind his back
without a trace of anger in their voices,
and thought: I probably say that sort of thing.

Chris Andrews

Writing a Dear John letter while reading Abraham and Torok*

Dear [insert name here],

You have eaten me
(a me that stands in for another that is).
They call it incorporation.

You swallowed me deep in your belly of
unsobbable sobs, of
unsayable to be saids
in your belly of rotting sugar.

You kept me on a chain
like a pet
       you starve
at the door of the crypt (of your child mother).
They call you a cryptophore, a poem, a poet.
They dare to re-write Hamlet and I dare to re-write you.

Of course the secret,
not just any secret,
not just *a* secret,
but a tomb, an enclave, a haunting …

your grandmother God in her cardigans
giving you the gaps, giving you the fear,
the wordless passing of the baton
of shame, of shame
and the silence of corpses screaming.
They call it the phantom.

I want out your belly love,
to stand with Hamlet in an ending re-imagined,
in an ending where
only the dead
    are buried.

Meera Atkinson

---

* The collected essays of the Hungarian-French analysts and theorists Nicolas Abraham and Maria Torok were published in *The Shell and the Kernel* (Vol. 1, University of Chicago Press, 1994). Abraham and Torok fused philosophy, psychology, linguistics and literary theory to posit their unique view of trauma, with particular focus on transgenerational transmission. Their work has been described as a 'poetics of hiding' and a significant development that pays homage to Freudian psychoanalytic theory while offering a radical critique.

What a Pencil Can Do

Is nothing a word is unable. To undo a twisted knot, holding a
fridge to the truck, I begin drawing. I draw for two hours. You
might understand from elementary maths, or the wild oddity
of a softball in the hand compared to that of a tennis ball,
that patterns are solved by our bodies. (I can sleep through
the night beside my lover our bodies so thin in the same place
they forget to discern – Picasso was never patient with a pencil.
Her Bonnard body beside me.)

If you unable a word from itself it becomes a sword. If you
unable a word from its shelf – feminine and utterly herself – it
moved unnoticed in her mouth. When unable to wake we have
to bite each other, or *bit* appeared at the end of a sharpening.
Looking for a sharpening during lovemaking. The thud, a
through-light from the blinds. Blind. A pencil is utterly blind.
Is what it can do.

Luke Beesley

Flower Stall

from Devadatta's poems

Whenever I come to Sarnath,
I hope that I can beg in the artisans' quarters so I can watch
the garland-makers' daughters. Now, I watch them
cup their fingers round the flowers, twist the stems
and draw the threads up with long bare sweeps

of their arms. I dream
they harvest me, nectar me, flavour me with the pollen-scented
fingers they wipe across their hair, down their bodices,
over their breasts. I dream their mouths festoon mine.

In Sarnath, no matter
what stern monk is with me on my rounds, no matter
what precepts or verses I'll recite, I know I'll never
stop wishing my face and robes can be stained not with mud,
or common potter's clay; not with spills of gruel,

or curd, or ghee;
not with fruit, or grease, or drips of whey; not with daubs
of honey, or splotches of spice, but with the smears and
    smutches
from each garland-maker's daughter's fecund fingers.

Judith Beveridge

Ground Swell

from Devadatta's poems

So many insects clicking, jumping up against my legs
        with the torsional stress of little springs.
   So many mouths dressing the flax,
the scutch, quitch and barley, corn and sesame;
     so many mouths
         in a chirl and chirm.
   I can hear them all in a tidal race
     over sweet flag and gale, sorghum and sorrel;
    insects eating away petals
      and grain heads,
     hanging on in a swirl of wind, hanging on
as the tails of mules
       come at them
  like the swippling swishes of fly-maddened flails.
         They scritch from the briar tangles,
   from leaves and twigs; all around I hear the scrape
   of their winnowing legs.

So many insects
     loose in the wind, loose in the grasses,
loose in the mustard, loose in the thistles and furze;
   poised, then shifting – a blur, a flurry
      over witch hazel,
        hyssop, trillium and mallow –
  a transient halo that's cropping my head.

Judith Beveridge

Yasodhara

from Devadatta's poems

At night I think of her hair like a free hoard
of honey in my hands. Sometimes, I imagine she is letting
me thread jasmine, or strips of perfumed bark through her hair;
that I'm rolling her hair into a thick bun at her nape,
dressing it with oil, or adorning it with feathers.

Sometimes, I dream she lets me colour her parting
with the same vermillion stick she'll later apply to her lips.
I think of her hair and I smell leaf musk, myrrh,
then the peregrine rain. When insects fizz and snap
at the lamplight, I dream they are the sound of the teeth

of one of her ivory combs, breaking as I draw them
down those heavy strands, the light stroking,
then filling her hair with shadow. When the days
and nights pass with unremitting rain, I dream I hear the sighs
of her bracelets slipping into my secret whisperings

of her name. But some nights, all I can hear is her
cracking in half all of her gem-studded combs; then the rasp
and harrow of the stone-handled knife: Yasodhara
hacking her hair back to her scalp – the *flump* of it falling –
and Yasodhara sobbing out Siddhattha's name.

Judith Beveridge

The Blind Minotaur

Pablo Picasso, Vollard Suite, plate 97

Night's the ground beneath my feet
since I learned to walk with you.
Scented guide with birds and flowers on your breath,

it's no earth, but a sea we walk across.
These sailors, pulling out from shore,
delivered our desertion.

In this new life of mine,
my heart keeps coming on
its every old error, grassed over

as if natural convexities,
the quickly earthed parts of who I am,
underground until the brass of a song

blew in a resurrection mood.
I'd have eaten you alive, girl,
had you come to me trembling around the spiral wall,

dust closing on your fingertips: and then.
Now your eyes are my dominion
which your feet traverse directly,

and your fingers are the chords that stagger me.

Judith Bishop

Brief Life

Alone Sunday
having caught

the last of the
Ray Davies documentary,

tears in my eyes.
Still, standing

tears, not crying –
thinking, gratefully,

how good
the credits are:

silent, no image –
which gives me time

to turn the telly off
before the ads –

& smile, at some of the
English names

Rugge-Price,
somebody-Hicks.

I think, *Mervyn Hicks*, a great
footballer I used to love, his

bulk moving like
'Waterloo Sunset' down

the field, dummying.

I think I saw him do it once
till he got close enough

for a drop goal.
(He missed, wonderfully.)

And then I think
Susan Mervyn-Jones. Ray

has peformed 'Waterloo Sunset':
life is a dream

'whenever they look at
Waterloo sunset / they are in

Paradise' – Terry &
Julie, the young

clerical workers in Davies' song.
Susan was my first

girlfriend – or I
wanted her to be.

I held her once, dancing.

I still remember
the heat of her body,

the smell of her hair.
A beautiful person,

small, dark. She died
a teenager, suffering

an asthma attack
while pulling

tight clothes on
over her head

suffocated. Life.
is short, Ray Davies says.

I think of Viv Miller,
last night – how good it's been

to have seen her
over these last years.

Cath rings, from Alice,
where she is.

The Todd River
is flowing it rained

so much last night.
A duck – or pigeon is it? –

sits near the river's edge.
Home tomorrow.

The dog is okay
after her operation,

Anna & Chris I
saw last night briefly –

they seem okay –

I'm not going to Penelope's
(Cath agrees).

Home tomorrow.

I play some Dave Holland,
move around the house

doing things, picking up,
tidying, straightening –

inside, outside – time
like an element around me.

Ken Bolton

Summer Day

(reading a Cuban poem while waiting at the pathologist)

Not words on a page
but an old man opposite me
who is whispering –
his life, the furniture, the stars,
the kitchen clatter, all
appear in the air around him as he talks,
this voice that touches each thing
to verify exactly where it stands.
The tropic sun is bright and all-consuming
inside and outside the poem.
It is quiet enough to recognise his voice quite clearly.
I too am dying.
Beyond the circle of his speech
one undivided silence sustains and engulfs me:
the summer sky, Cuba walking on across the page,
my suspect blood.

Peter Boyle

Towns in the Great Desert (2)

The size of tall-masted ships,
of a spire of prayer,
the gate of hammered earth
and nailed wooden planks
is wheeled shut at second watch.
Guards wield huge feral dogs on iron chains
while other dogs laze about unchained
to supervise late arrivals.

The last to make his way through the closing gates,
he drags himself with the stumps of his arms,
battered legs trailing over stony ground.
Each night he sleeps in an old car,
turns the motor to a slow hum, climbs
into the engine, curls up beside its warmth,
locks the bonnet behind him.
His skin at dawn has the black fragrance of oil.
Each day he stretches out on the beach
to be pounded clean by the surf.
His body has the purple glow
of finely tuned mallets.

In the sky of this town there are no passing clouds or stars,
only the unbroken wall of millennial dust.
Sea water is all there is
to cook, to bathe, to wash.
To buy water to drink
they send their children to slave in distant mines.
Of this town they say
'The gods never came here.'

Peter Boyle

Alibi at the Start of Summer

In backwards, sea spray thinning ash as the city
turns from itself, the ocean that brought it faces off
a dying Westerly, bushfire winds clipping sprawled
edges of suburbia where Alibi Wednesday lets slip her
need for understanding of this kind or another.
Jumbo miles away caring for their father, his monologues
engines for survival that splutter to life in aftermath.
Alibi had been hoarding for years, out there her gathering
hunger, half-hearted aching, heady with glue-sniffing,
the primitive clutching of the boys, gathering up accounts,
instants of ingratitude, the overall lack of graciousness,
salt-laced crest and crumble of bodies, waves mimicking
freakish winds and seasonal change, determining
which way illumination shed. Fifteen years is a lifetime.
You could suffocate, taking it in too deeply so she learnt
to bark and hawk. She feels like the city, backed up
against the sea, dusk cornered and for once turning around,
capering headlands, licking names as she twists newspaper
into curlicues of flame and presses against stripped skin
of eucalypts, scraggle ends of underbrush and banksia dry
and tindered, translating flickering dark to daylight,
rough and immediate.

Michael Brennan

Rats, Lice and History*

This morning, making coffee, I watched
through the kitchen window an old crow
settle on a low branch of a Blue Mountains ash and,
looking out over the valley, for no
apparent reason, burst into raucous song,
and I thought – I don't know why – of that other
late summer, so long ago, when,
full of my mother's death
I set out with five hundred new-
earned dollars, a camera and a haversack
heavy with volumes of Jack Kerouac
and took flight for the northern winter, to visit
school-friends of two years before – landing
in Los Angeles, heading for San Diego
to see the best of them, then
betraying him, only five days later, when,
at her invitation, I went to visit his
girlfriend, four hundred miles north
and left sex raw and sleepless the next morning
by Greyhound for Iowa and the parents
of the first girl I had ever made love with, whose
doctor-father (she was now at school elsewhere) regaled me
all evening with *Rats, Lice and History* before
(such perfect irony) I woke itchy and sore
in his attic guest-bed with new-
hatched Australian crab-lice of my own
and, confessing, was shown the door
with stony silence and a prescription for DDT, his
attempt, I think, to kill me, though I went on, still
burning, physically, to see

and be rebuffed by his daughter in Milwaukee
and so hastened home to my once-
host-family in Chicago, for three days of rest
before heading for Rochester and the photographs
of Weston and Cameron and Minor White
and a once-dreamt-of night
with Miss Teenage Illinois of four years before,
who sent me, then, to stay with her cousin in Baltimore
who, undeterred by the thought
of her heart-surgeon husband,
would wake me each morning with languid
strokings on the floor – even her name now
lost in the subsequent embarrassment of my telephone call
from a clinic, in St John, Newfoundland, run
by Sadists of some Christian order
who had burned and scalded and punctured me,
to tell her of what was almost certainly (but
wasn't) a cousin-to-cousin STD, and then – my true
goal all along – after another eight days' travelling,
to M., in Oregon, ten years older than I, who had once, in Sydney,
held me so long and so gently, seeing
something I had not yet seen in me,
and we made love at last,
fumbling and sad, in the bleak snow-light,
while her writer partner was out,
and she came, and sobbed, and since no-one
had ever come with me before, I thought
I had hurt or broken her: 'It's
alright,' she said, 'It's alright,'

but it never was, not for another thirty years yet, not
until you and I met, and the wheel
left me, here, in this openness, on a
morning like this one, trying like that
old crow to sing it out, let it all
go, the pain and the confusion and the
embarrassment of it, the regrets and the
damage and the stubborn, un-
trackable grieving, into this sudden light.

David Brooks

---

* Hans Zinsser, *Rats, Lice and History* (1935)

Mary Shelley's Man

singed
and restless stretched   lulled father's casting
womanhood   caterwauling fevers, death and the
joined to creature knowing
not born

black dank cold break with clouds
rush of consciousness confound
with the ache and throb of
life   stitches   blue/green/yellow/red
bruises' kisses everywhere

black dank cold river mirror split
like paper down the ark of him
words will him to believe
black the warm thrump-thump of Percy's chest
snap man this head rusted with clouds
and the blood break hands
lumbered out

Dada's mirror children
eaters of gently trailed fire
when he came
she knew –
corpse scent
open grave part fire
his smell, rush of consciousness
confounded with the age   bonggggggggggggggg
mist rolling on –
her in her wooden wheels and bells echoing tolling
cold ink-stained hands defied
the fingertips trailed gently came

this head rusted with clouds
and the blood break hands
joined to him groan of sky-bolted by a storm tearing
mountain pain
half-sunk, his head rusting
joined to him her fingertips tearing
joined to him by a storm of ice

Jen Jewel Brown

Spirulina to go

if you haven't been lost
        at the showground,
in the bush,   in Westfield Plaza,
                on an island

you may not know
            the perpetual present
        is exhausting,

way too many
        concurrent points of view,

– something too <u>free</u> in aleatory –

and further,
            a burden –   a century
        of hortatory Stcinisms,
Yes, that's how I read it –

                famously, she says
'a sentence is not emotional, a paragraph is'

the 'difficult' Stein at her best

    'Think carefully of nouns.
    Vary and think very think very once
    and once more of a noun a noun they like'

DRINKING STRAW –   there's your noun, mrs!
                hope you like it

*

discussing Immaculate Conception
on the landline
&
Original Sin –
who *knows* what it is?

does an individual matter?
(immeasurable)

*

boys own rumbles by
on a rusted bicycle
ruining the dawn's bleak dream,
the flattened one,
where you emerge from the lake
and wave, almost languidly

*

there's the dribbling bronze boar
outside Sydney hospital,
its nose shiny from stroking

dwelling
on isolation (don't dwell)
and other sad feelings (shouldn't dwell)
like a detainee in this,
the inadequate body

red bumps
bigger than goosebumps –
but not exactly pimple size
more weals than whelks

who can understand the nurse
    when she phones
        with the laboratory test data?

*

No-one ever here, no footpath crowd,
  every knock of a hinge is creepy
     crack of a floorboard,
           rustle and gust

perhaps it's revelatory,
     or will be

can the past catch up with you

*

problem –   how to begin the music,
        harder than beginning a poem?

the ringtone
     was the sound of that decade

if you just keep turning up
       on time

 eventually

     might rain photons

*

that'd be good

*

you're embarrassed
           by my slurp
when I'm
           guzzling spirulina
                 but
I've been to my personal best
           and back –
     I'm not worried

*

early intervention buys time,

how much is time these days?
           (a cheap question)

*

if you see something
           say something –

This is *everything I could want*
                in a lifetime of products

*

pulling on another shirt
      over two shirts
as weather
      sets in

standing in the clothes
           that you once wore

*

hours sitting in one spot

a rosella fell, lodged dead in the branches,
        I took it down
    and buried it behind the begonia

       a new cicada began to chirr

*

I've been coasting,
      a clown visiting a conservatorium,

   time now for application

I want to reach the inhumans,
    find the kind of poetry
              that appeals to them,
to their original intelligence,
     and then,
struck by enargia, Propriety Limited is us

*

Unable to afford
     the G'Day Highway Motel,
  I sleep in a car in its shadow

while

the town that makes
    the world's supply
     of plastic drinking straws
  is booming

*

the dendrite moves slowly
        towards the synapse –
    arrives two weeks later

    WISHING YOU
A SPEEDY RECOVERY

    the light here is so dim

*

an indestructible host organism
        has the softest touch

strike another match, go start anew

Pam Brown

Fuel

You asked to stop there for a can of coke, you needed to piss
and the tank was empty so I pulled in. I stood by the bowser
pumping gas to fuel dreams set on fire years before and you
said to the attendant that you'd been short changed.

If only you knew the truth in that.

The tyres were near-bald and paint job robbed by rust and we
were there ten metres apart, sliding doors between us and I
was standing watching your mouth move.

You were telling the attendant that there were not enough
coins – the change was wrong – and you were pleading with
your eyes with one hand in your front pocket looking casual
and honest.

And you looked at me through the glass and back at him and
you picked at lint from your stained pullover.

I watched your mouth.

You were hoping like fuck that he'd give you that two-dollar
coin so you could walk through those sliding doors, flip that
piece, lay it on the dash, shove your feet up and feel just a little
richer for all those years we'd spent.

Allison Browning

from 'crevice' a mnemonica

I. NO DOUBT ABOUT IT

i read doris lessing in delphi
short stories on the oregano trail –
then the bronze charioteer asked
me out for dinner, i forgot to say
no; at chandigarh i drank
six bottles of limca as a man
breathed under sand near the
bus station for a rupee, a town
where the bank ran out of money
for thirty minutes   then i bought
'coolie' to read under my room
fan   the postcards vanished
into the wall; i noticed god
hastening down the hill
by the river at rishikesh afraid
of being recognised –
i wore time like a birthday
there was no one to tell me
what to do –

II. CHORUS

a morning of false
fiancées, you fluked
a pose till the salad
dazzled like a coup;

the celebration at
epidaurus, sunset
medea; the guards
in white hats circled
the horde of stones,
suspicious of anything
restless in the air –
it was raucous awe
and postcards by midnight
you were all as young
as those rusty odes

III. SOAKED

the well, full of gossip and
whisper, myths got confused
in the hangovers everyone had
nicknames it was our map to
the lore, a dramatis personae
for the cognac sippers in
the siesta we played
their role in our awkward
holiday like gauche puppets,
the empty barn a dark treasury
for what could not be named;
joyce's ulysses got soaked in
red wine the waves broke in
a hard currency on the shore –
the wooden slats saved our feet
from a hot sand's intolerance we
took the bargain option of slipping into
the murky lagoon; the relique windmill
way above the ocean was our talisman
and obrigad how we flew –

IV. PLINTH

a boat eating a rock's history
too much sun in your diary
things scar your pockets like
awkward souvenirs; the hand
me down visa fades into another
century the secret of the retsina
rotting old photographs   still here
with a donkey load of memories you
don't know what to do with, the more
prepositions you manufacture the more you
encourage them like a clamour of bees

V. KIDNEY

the belly replied to
the seafood like a diva
a new music swayed in
the lemongrass – sheets crackled
and smelt as they should in a
velvet hotel the key napped
in its pearly shell: you
could hardly believe this
invocation; a private swim
in a private pool, kidney
shaped intimacy a tropical
garland of neon plants
and the dust of delhi dispersed

a travel magazine is redundant
research – pineapple princess breezes
through the foyer to the aqua tour
bus, james bond island stunned
like a camera: the tick of
buddha thought in the third
dark cave amplified those days –

Joanne Burns

Child

for Alex Domaille

At thirteen if she closes her eyes
standing, she topples – she can't walk down stairs –
her wobbling gait, knees sagging in
like a marionette, grows worse, is diagnosed:

vertebra buckled, pressing its cord,
six weeks to paralysis. So hospital – hours
of the white ceiling, electric thoughts
of the heart and breath on the monitor – she comes back

in a padded plastic brace, a black metal raven
roosting on her shoulders, six kilos of bolts and screws
wrapping black wings about her golden hair –
what jocular surgeons call a 'halo'. She bares

the scar on her throat, draws her spine on the board
and talks us through. Half the class away at sport,
those left feel sick and want to cry,
the world at the whiteboard suddenly serious:

a change of tone in a parent's voice, life's voice.
To their faint questions, the whole torso
turns like a wobbling palanquin,
a Chinese opera warrior bearing

the weight of ritual, a head in stocks.
Face framed and locked, she explains
the finger-on-the-button of her bone's
perverse curve; the shave, the graft, how she sleeps

little, piled on pillows, parents turning her in shifts:
an excellent outcome, she goes home to wait out the weeks,
Baby Atlas shouldering the weight
of a child, too hard to hug, impossible to hold.

That year – new haircut, halo off, postponed, forgotten,
she wins the debate, sings over her project, 'Create
Your Own World'; colours, cuts and staples cardboard carefully.

Elizabeth Campbell

Dead Finish

In a few days the sea
   will have dried   up
                                     fine ruffled mangrove:
                                       rusted ditch, reef guts.
Less the rolling
turbine aw
of coast, gentle tidal wing –
                         more
the red ping of stretching lugger bellies,
flutes of scale   caving blue.

More, a sea of foothills where grasses end
               dead finish starts
                     to print the rubble, singing
granite dry. A few days further, hacks will grow into rockholes

    holding high the shapes of a clutching couple, a peering bust
                         calling light.
                             It comes running out of a crook
grasping anything in reach – bough, culvert, whistling feather,
    turns them stiff.
The valley basin will stretch, weeping up bright beds of shatter-
    cones and hairtail steps.
                                 It has dreamt of
light and dream around the corner; when light and dream crumble
    against one constant, grainy edge. Their rushing ovoid.
Tracing a bowl of rock to tears:
so, this is passage.

Bonny Cassidy

Lu Xun, your hands

But as you look up and inhale the intoxicating smoke from your tobacco,
can you spare a thought for those scrambling to find a way out of this nest
of scorpions?—XU GUANGPING, in her first letter to Lu Xun, 1925

Lu Xun, your hands
that you clasp behind your back,
across the black silk
of your scholar's dress. My eyes trace the length
of your fingers encircling your wrist. Tonight,
Lu Xun, your hands will drag
their heavy, eloquent path across
my milk-white skin. Your mouth will cease
to form words like *liberty, ideology,*
and *compassion* but will instead silently
enclose the peach blossoms
of my breasts

Lu Xun, your hands are the instruments
through which you conduct
your desires. In the morning, your fingers are pale
and controlled, your brush hovers
then descends upon the undulating sheets
of rice paper. My eyes follow only
each stroke. Your thoughts unfold before me, beginning
at the moss-green rocks. They linger
in the shade of the toothpick pavilion, beneath
its heavy jade tiles. They form a blood-red,
half-moon bridge

across the rush of river
fed by the waterfall whose origin lies
in the death-grey mountains. Lu Xun,
your hands warm the wood of the pipe
that I fill. My fingers, deft like birds
in flight, strike a match-soldier. Provoked,
it flares orange and ash. Dragon,
you exhale whole curlicues of cloud. Words
slumbering in my mind's recesses
now go up in smoke. They too know
that I am in heaven, Lu Xun,
for your hands

Eileen Chong

Sound Urn: Sonnet to Orpheus #5

Eric, tit-keening dank sty; lusty Rosa
knew hey-days; yah, Sue sigh, in gun-stained balloon.
Then all faces hissed: sigh Hermes, tar more foes, err
in demand! Damn weir-soul, Lenin's nicked moon,
human dray, harm men! Infer Guatemala
hissed, or flay us. Venice sinked, her common gate
is snicked. Shun feel. Vendredi rose in chaleur.
Ooh my Pa, target man's smell who bears state,
oh, free air swindles, moustache ears by grift!
Hunt when himself, hawk-banked dust, harsh wonder.
Indemn sign-wart, diss hear-sign who bears drift,
hiss her, her shone door to woe in ears' nicked bay. Light it,
dear liar, get her swanked! Him necked un-hander,
under cay hawked, under mare who bear trite It.

Justin Clemens

Yankunytjatjara Love Poems – English version

1.
I walk to the south
I walk to the north
where are you my Warrior?

I sit with the desert
I sit with the ocean
where are you my Warrior?

I sing to the trees
I sing to the rocks
where are you my Warrior?

I dance with the birds
I dance with the animals
where are you my Warrior?

Heaven is everywhere
where are You?

2.
I will show you a field of zebra finch Dreaming in the shadow
     of the *stony hill* ochre
when the soft blanket of language hums and kinship campfires
     flavour windswept hair

little girls stack single twigs on embers under *Grandfather's* skin
     of painted love
the dance of *emu* feathers will sweep the *red earth* with your smile

do not look at me in daylight; that gift comes in the night
tomorrow I will show *Mother* your marriage proposal in my smile

3.

in the cave she rolls *the big rock* for table, for *the desert wildflowers*
    they pick for one other
she carries *many coolamons* filled with river sand to soften the
    hard rock floor
she makes shelf from braided *saplings* to hold *all the feathers*
    given by the message birds
when he sleeps she polishes his weapons with goanna and emu
    fat till they glisten in fire light
he tells the story of the notches on his spear, the story of the
    maps on his *woomera*
their *eyes* fill with spot fires lit on his return
the other *women* laugh 'get over yourself' they laugh 'he's not
    that good'
she smiles she knows him in the night

4.

there is love in the wind by the singing rock
down the river by the ancient tree
love in *kangaroo goanna* and *emu*
love when spirits speak no human voice
at the sacred sites eyes unblemished
watch *wedge tail eagle* soar over hidden *water*
find the *love*

5.

Survival Day
I hear you as you sit
in silence your eyes search the Dreamtime
crammed in a modern world

Ah! there are the *children* of the Dreamtime
hands on thighs dancing
black legs beat drum and *didgeridoo*

Ah! there are the *Grandmothers* of the Dreamtime
quiet under shade trees alert for dangers
ready to fight protect and die

Ah! *husbands* and *wives* of the Dreamtime
share soul *celebrations* beyond the cultures
another *baby* of the Dreamtime will be born soon

Ah! *all the Grandfathers* sit silent
unmoving become rock face and sacred tree
the *gibar* magic man one with *the earth*

Ah! I see you on the horizon
in silence you search the Dreamtime
your *eyes* meet my silence

you reveal your presence with *your smile*

Ali Cobby Eckermann

Yankunytjatjara – a traditional Aboriginal language group of northwest
South Australia, who have maintained their traditional cultural prac-
tices and are a major language group of the Anangu Pitjantjatjara
Yankunytjatjara lands.

Bloom

Valle de Hurtado, Chile

As absurd as light:
my trying to savour these last days
of her last visit, my tossing like trees between the hours,
hopelessly turbulent,
her last filaments of presence dissolving
in a river hurtling towards an oceanic desert.

Still, those moments emerge
like water cupped in hands,
mountain water, frozen as futures,
their steely whiteness,
late afternoon sunlight slanting through membranes,
stumbling into shadows and recovering to bloom
in isolated pockets of shining terrain,
the oiled carving of an idle skink,
a careful puma's dark glass,
those voltaic moments purr like bows or hammocks,
her tanned skin and a thin book held open.

A sense – say it is of water on the tongue –
of a cool liquid circling around and into itself,
sliding into the darkness, negating itself
yet lacteal, sinuous, its glassy thickness – say
it is water on the tongue – clear, silken
liquid silent as memory,

a clearing sheltered by a maternal willow
and carried away by the river of an icy clock.

Stuart Cooke

3D Homer Simpson

for Rue

3D Homer Simpson is a collection of fragile card.
We punch him out of the frames with rigid thumbs –
blue pants, white shirt, yellow skin. Each flat piece
is a strange butterfly revealed as it simply folds
into long leg columns and square stomach panels
representing his Duff-fuelled curves. Peering inside
he is a blueprint pattern of dots and alphabetised tabs.
B fits with B, K with K, as if to remind us of our
nucleotide matches. It is a fine script within us
and six years ago you arrived so neatly packaged.
Each day now is for deciphering yourself transcribed
among the language of others. The silences filled
with hollow catchphrases worth the joy of their repetition.
Don't you look like your sisters! You hear that a lot –
the mystery of your own insides. When you go to bed
you see colourful fonts blooming beneath your eyelids.
I am swearing in the kitchen, sticking myself, the last bits
into place. All I have left are these thin strands of hair.
It is true we are falling apart. Cliché perhaps, still
the creases are tested, dots of glue coming unstuck.
When I present him in the morning you say
he looks like me and I chase you *why you little*
holding you tight, this typical pose spelling –
happy birthday for yesterday.

Nathan Curnow

Cutter Sutra

'... But enough about me; how do you think I look?'

I was always on my mind. It's not a compliment.
Amen to the Thunderbolt in the Dark Void.
I opened my eyes & it was called peeking.
The stars could still be thrown for sport back then.
Gamboling and cavorting, fleece shot through by lightning,
the insipid lamb of awakening learned the ur-Parable:
Burnt Lamb looks like a lamb, but when you blow, *puff!*
there is nothing there; one more lamb out of way of self
leads the world closer to its own self-realisation.
God designed geology and quasars without prior context
and had no idea we'd be so long about it. Shortcomings
were long-goings because they took an awful long time
to go, *boom-boom*. Little thunders in black time
licking us up: O the slurp of the ages and I am gone –
to some place home besides me calling you back
like a little bird *herc herc*. I dreamed I saw, florid
with taxonomic pain, a sulphur-crested scarlet-breasted
grey-tailed pygmy toucan, from which waking was
a somewhat time-elasticised relief; I planted seeds
in oceans long ago, apparently concurrent with the belief
I was a pond. (More lately I took on the mask of water.)
O how it flew, the night: blizzarded with the prepositions
of mineness, take me a woman, cry me a river, let it
either 'all hang out' or 'be'. But as for language
I had no desires, other than I must be protected
from it and its. Game theory kept the world on its toes.
Jive talk filled in the rest with misfortunate infelicities.
On Walking Rain Road the rain man came again all
spectral and muddy. I wondered fervently what I was
waiting for. Not the lunatic search for the everyman lost,

surely not. That was language at best, aflame through
twists and turns, while we died. Everything's all right:
things are crashing down, but uptight, not uptown.
I learned the art of feasting from time spent on highways:
a fine art, as they go. Highways ride on cycles then get
buried beneath new highways. I've got a feeling geologists
know this, deeply, but feelings aren't facts. Of course,
laughter then disavows and disinters the sedimentary layers
or the concepts they make up which (run together) get called
life. Burnt string looks like a string but the action of wind
cleans all, and self. Give me some time to blow the man down.

Luke Davies

Eventide

'Too often, it seems, they do not understand
why we resist (against all reasoning)
that other world which lies so near at hand:
a room with one of the family, the *sensible* thing,
or a Sunset Retirement Centre, replete with friends,
medical staff, social activities, bus trips, all
the many comfortable ways in which our ends
(and *theirs*, of course) can be accomplished by the small
surrender of living *here*, where home says what we *are*,
lit, as it may be, by the evening star ...

So small a sacrifice (you'd think!) and yet
so large and threatening a one for us,
who have so many losses to regret
when we're so aware we're near the terminus.

We sadly shake our heads: from where we live
can they not see that this or that *new* move
could be, *would* be so definitive,
and that although they come to offer with love
an alternative life, so much that's gone
now calls us to honour that lost past
which made us what we are, and later on
will, like a new-found lover, hold us fast?

Those other futures which they hold before us
can never tempt us and are bound to fail,
even though they plead in caring, sharing chorus
– gently but firmly (or with tooth and nail)
we must forego them to that final day
when whatever we have left is taken away.'

Bruce Dawe

Sweeping

Nearly every time I take the shortcut down this
curving street I see you, sweeping the grassy verge
outside your home or doggedly chasing a single leaf.

You're always in curlers with a scarf tied round them
and wearing something that looks like the seersucker
brunch coat my grandmother made me when I was nine.

I want to sit us on the ground, lean you back against
my knees, remove the scarf, take out the curlers
one by one and loose each curl with tender fingertips,

then take the hands that grip the broom and say, *Come on,
let's paint the town! Go dancing, drink cocktails, smoke cigars,
take coffee at a rakish hour* ... We'd come home as the sun

crept up and with the broom I'd gather leaves to make
a crisp lush bed where we would take our pleasures, my
fingers in your curls for all the neighbourhood to see.

Tricia Dearborn

Holiday

for Dorothy

Our son pisses on the rental carpet & Dot Porter dies.
In the casuarinas, snagged, red lures hang like obscene
Christmas baubles, as fairy martins ascend into angels.
A Brahminy kite rotates over the khaki water, its dark
Undercarriage slaps the estuary, but comes up empty.
It's so like that, hit & miss in the majestic river mouth
As a Sun god out of control ignites its auburn feathers.
Everything we catch this day we release, a black bream
Lives to refract more light; silver scales a hard exchange
As primary school kids begin to reel in the sudden past.
We even let the dead bait go; some odds we try to even.
My daughter, all of four, writes the letters of her name
In Chambers Island's sand; a swell extinguishes them
On this holiday, as her words move out with the tide.

B.R. Dionysius

Guillemots

There's an intruder
in the cliff city
of the guillemots,
a seeker for eggs
of various speckled
greens and blues.
The stunt exists
to show us in our lounge rooms
how much the Saxons
prized this protein.
You're just home.
I feel relieved
that you haven't
been scaling such heights,
even though you did
steal the indeterminate
colour of your eyes
from these lofty clutches.
You're just home
with the slightest reprimand
from your grandparents –
for wearing the wrong clothes –
suspended on the air,
a television sea bird's call,
that diminishes now
as you turn those eyes to mine.
You do not stop looking at me.
I stroke your cheek
recalling a radio voice from the past:

they called it their tender time.
I reclaim you by this gaze,
your first gift to me,
and I know you by colour
as a guillemot mother
exhausted from hunting
can return to her own eggs, hers alone,
in the vast sea-bird citadel
on the high white cliffs.
There are no raiders yet
and you can wear
all the wrong clothes you want.
Beyond your cradled shoulder
I keep the intrepid egg thief
at a blurry distance.

Lucy Dougan

The Exeter Book

or, as Lee had it
                    a hand
from a cloud, grasp-
ing
a pint?

sooty gulls preen
on the Exe,
geese
            ('you wouldn't want
            one of those flying into you'
            the impaired man

he's absolutely right

those hills beyond the A377
down the bottom of the street

a wind, almost
Atlantic

in a bar with
the Unofficial Roy Fisher
                        opposite
Gibson's Plaice
(fishmongers)
                above it (improbably)
an Australian flag

                    DOVER SOLE
        SCALLOPS   BRILL
            DABS   TURBOT
                WILD TROUT

Topsham, the bridge
over the muddy Exe,
Dutch gables,
'Georgia on my mind'

upstairs, in the quiet
of The Ship, windows
view a wall, a
ventilator calligram:

ʘ ʘ ʘ ʘ ʘ ʘ
ᴖ ᴖ ᴖ ᴖ ᴖ ᴖ

white paint
obscures the rest

the back of a man, sculpted
on a chair, a mansard,
hedges in distant fields

the rumble below
of Exeter Central

sun beats down on the fenced off
Royal Albert Memorial Museum

in 2011: 'all will be revealed'

Laurie Duggan

Roman Road

A proud infant who will not cry,
the air stuffed full of *it's not fair,*
rumours of flood elsewhere in Poplar,
Plumstead, Lewisham. Not here,

though one dribbled blade slashes
the side mirror, its dots excitable as men
I once saw tracking gold on the Fosse Way.
Gluttons for drought, they lacked society

to give their store of interests ease,
dabbled with circuits, AC/DC, failed
almost universally. Maybe they found
what they were looking for in God

who isn't there and never was and so
cannot be lost. A few spots more, more
and still more. The strident pylons hum
approvingly, *fall in, hail Caesar!*

Will Eaves

The House of Time

And fleetingly it seemed to him
That in between one eye blink and the next
Time paused, allowing time to be installed
Within that countless interim,
Coiled up, on hold,
A memory predicted and recalled.
Now, that weak muscle flexed,
All that contained him started to unfold

In front of him, a moving book
In three dimensions he could wander through,
At will, at any point, now, since, before,
To feel, to listen and to look –
A house, or suite
Of rooms around a circling corridor,
And waiting there, he knew,
Were all the peopled days he'd not repeat.

Slowly he stretched his hand to open
The first door on his right. Why, this was easy:
Christmas when he was seven, and his aunt
Playing a polonaise by Chopin,
Badly. 'Lenore,
We know you think you can, dear, but you can't.'
And he was resting, queasy
From too much pudding. Now, another door:

So far, so faint, not yet an I,
A pulse of sense, he hung upon a web
Of knitted blood. Above, the muffled heart
Performed its mindless lullaby
And in the womb
He slept on half-awake. That was his part
Elsewhere, too, at the ebb
Of his last consciousness. Another room:

He recognised at once the face
Of one who five years hence he would have bound
As closely to him as a Siamese twin.
How recklessly he would replace
That loving care.
Absorbed, now, in the dream of skin on skin,
He whispered the profound
And destined promises she'd never share.

He shuddered, shut it, and proceeded.
So room on room, all of his scenes, arranged
In simultaneous succession, played
Before him, unignored, unheeded,
Each a *tableau*
Vivant and drama, driven and yet stayed,
Developing, unchanged.
At last the time that paused for time to flow

He saw was coming to an end.
He saw himself before himself, distinct
As when – a life ago – it came to him
A single blink could comprehend,
And then unfold,
All time within that countless interim.
He blinked. And then he blinked.
And time continued as it coiled, on hold.

Stephen Edgar

Guileless

Marilyn often made love in the afternoon
standing up
                        to the studio bosses
she was like an apparition
                                        a body in distress
whose skin
                        stopped her going naked
under the bright lights
                                        they were waiting
she was always late
                        you wait
therefore you love me
                        and I cannot
be replaced
                        when she arrived
the vomiting goddess
                                        felt a fake
coming on
                you know how people
feel about themselves
                        a phony
tearing her skin off
                                        strip by strip
when night fell
                        she talked about
Joe who sometimes hit her
                                        saying
I have a gay side
                        a sad side too

and want to disappear
                    she knew
that she could *be* someone
                        only by being
someone else
                    between 'take' and 'cut'
there was little to distinguish
                            what she
didn't understand
                        from what she
stood for
                e.g. Rilke, Faulkner,
Steinbeck, Freud
                            Death
it springs out of nowhere.

Chris Edwards

A Passenger from the Childhood House

The sheen on things under blue
and the cool acreage of canary
light has not a hint of crimson

till you drive me home
with the idea of sky over the bay.
Save tomorrow, the poster says,

from things that eat organs, things
that multiply in vessels, cells
skimming the venous and arterial

roads. (The careful knife
under the skin prises, cleaving
the old idea and the good)

Nanna can smell the rain
coming; she scents the hunger
of the soil. When my surfaces are raw

and ragged, like a tree shedding,
I wander in memory. The past
tastes bitter and lovely

(don't stitch me up too soon)
The flame tree blooms
blood in the childhood yard.

A mask slips. Forgiveness
is neither random nor chosen.
New rain yaps on the roof,

the wipers scatter recollection,
intermittent with the light. Grace
throws itself into my lap

and licks my face. When it lands
on me, what can I do but laugh
at once wary and delighted.

Anne Elvey

What is a Soul?

A soul quivers
in the palm of your
voice, is still when
a sparrow alights

outside. In the winter
sun a soul
twitches neck and
head, neck

buried in the pulse
of a round & thinking
flesh. Like any feathered
thing in its space

it does not try
to be noticed. A soul
pauses to witness
a magpie. Its body

is a lever, its
beak a chisel,
prising bark from the trunk
of a myrtle. On the sky

a soul writes
itself. Winter
tosses a gauze
across the single crescent

jewel that fades
into day, watermark
of the fingernail that
lifted a scab. Then

the soul is a prayer
may a great
white egret
lance your skies.

Anne Elvey

It appears we are machines

It appears we are machines to manufacture words,
each weighted with deliberation or floating crosswise
on currents of uncertainty. Sea birds swoop,
plunge through an interlocking edge, come away
with wriggling fish between their beaks or nothing,
either way a penetration of that collusion,
surface-glued-to-surface, which signals difference,
one side, the lean, light-strutted transparency of flight,
the other a greyscale, ever-deepening dark: at best
a hard-won buoyancy. Lie back, you say, trust
the density of matter, the way the sun can warm
even as the sea enfolds you in a cool embrace:
displacement, though it almost feels like home.
Words leave. Air and water rush to fill the space.

Brook Emery

Proviso

Cento for Election Day

And I heard my Coleridge say, 'I am
the patron saint of everyone who died
before you.' Had to carry a torch,
a hunger you'll never show.
Under alien skin 16A and B
I bring my body through
this mortal world, American town
founded on a hologram. This *matter-
of-fact free house*, this one nightmare
reaching out to consume you.
Driving down Broadway
I told my child: it was never yours,
only a naming call, pitched their tents
& destroyed whole nations
eight miles from here. What?
We live in a burning sideline,
same old fetch. We do this landscape
crowned and slow. At the crossroads
I mutate into a flower that blooms
once every 25 years. Words
large enough to contain you: during,
pine, upend, the eating of men.

Kate Fagan

wide open road

There could be anything.... elongation of a spear.

Needled To a sphere they think, mind suffused with
honey, i reach out, hes a dead man,
closing the gateness behind him.

We crack the nut & Go on – Theres Ballet in the trees
What a Cool Idea, the economy flows Like a creek
at our feet, with a few subtle body bags we ignore.

Then i realise im not wearing my red
Pin or singing

"How do you think it feels at night!"
It gives you a bad back
& a youthless appearance

Sleeping with people or sheep dogs

When the loneliness you love is in the
Eyes of someone else youre wired

   We came back after a decade of
   Drought the briar & burdock gone trialling new forms of
   Outdoor glass – the schools are laying eggs now

Our vehicle stops

We sit on our tails

Some get pads out
Draw a blue sky

   Reflectors on the inside....

You touch a locust & have a vision
That were
Walking along a rope not

A-road the koalas Yaaawnnnnnn
For the money
Nurses cruise through pursued by reporters on trikes.

Michael Farrell

Flute of Milk

after John Banville's The Sea

Inside the dairy, washed so white
it approaches blue,
muslin-draped pans of milk
dream in their silence
and two steel milk-churns
(sentries in flat hats)
burn with white rosettes –
light held from the sun.
I remember the butter churn –
the handle I never turned.
Memory prefers to hold things still,
but the past, present and future
are a long flute of milk.
I am washing my hands: a spot
on the curve of the hand basin
streams out like a distant nebula.
I remember washing her hair –
pouring water from a jug.
The sluice fell on the crown of her head.
Beads broke in a silver string,
like the bracelet around her wrist,
that lit diadem of our night swim.
The water flowed and flowed over our arms,
as though undulations of black satin.

She stands unshadowed now
in milky light – her face
seems almost featureless
as if the profile of a coin.
Be anyone you like she said.
But who, if not ourselves, are we?
Is a rose red in the dark?
I wash some colour here, scumble
a detail there. Her portrait will never be done.

Susan Fealy

Metamorphosis

for Franz Kafka, 1883–1924

Cathedral-bird cawdaw jackerdaw,*
a dark plumaged passerine bird.
A jackdaw is *kavka* in Czech.

The genus of crows and ravens,
it calls in a metallic *chyak chyak*.
Cathedral-bird cawdaw jackerdaw.

Jackdaws are harbingers of rain,
their under-wings are wire grey,
and *kavka* means jackdaw in Czech.

His sisters Elli, Valli and Ottla
died in forty-one, two and three.
Cathedral-bird cawdaw jackerdaw.

Greeks tell that a jackdaw falls
seeking his kin in a dish of oil.
A jackdaw is *kavka* in Czech.

His beak and throat are clattering:
he calls in a metallic *chyak chyak*.
Cathedral-bird cawdaw jackerdaw.
A jackdaw is *kavka* in Czech.

Susan Fealy

---

* Some obsolete names for 'jackdaw'

Think Act

for Tucker

still a prima donna maradona soars
the hand of god seems as unlikely as hess
the sick swan descends sans plan and
it's easy to get marooned behind the lines
say goodnight to itaewon's bum fluff gis
tumble down hooker hill bright lights fried mandu
wankered in a cab through the window
the mantra of apartments and pork signs
across the han seoul is cyber punk memories
in the fugitive drizzle a thoroughbred gallops
across the cabbie's fake timber dash
straddle the hill the blood of walker's men
scrubbed clean by roulette wheels and daiquiris
abandoned at the back of beyond
pissing on a power pole in the jackie howe dawn
when the monsoons come there is time for rest
rivers where the banks chaperoned streams
sweeping ssangyongs through drainage ditches
at home on the telly korean newlyweds
roadtripping through alice a eurobeat
skinny tie b-grade with ponytail
a getaway in a stolen souped up xu-1
that was the eighties nobody stayed for the dailies

Liam Ferney

War Through the TV

Even the bombs aren't enough,
the words you use heated with
agitation becoming mild with
repetitive fillers and sequenced
segues, the sensational imaginings
of someone missing under rubble,
the flight of a missile that whines
and wings and plummets into
firecracker glow behind you as
you frame your pictures with
references un-meted so that
sadness lurches and shimmers
but inevitably pales. It is the one
you can't perform on account, the
one that draws a cachet to the eye
and only a feather to the mind that
is the most re-sellable, the
imagined real, the un-win-able
war, every unsinkable ideology
which holds it up overexposed so
that any palm you may extend
is given like a leaking boat.

S.J. Finn

Manipulation Modifies Your Structures

Verbal communication is what we like
Verbal knowledge is what we like
Reading ability is talking we like
Our components of language is stronger
Than criteria type trends
Our vocabulary is a mixed world over
Our new trend co-existences are words in medium spirits
Formation comes from techniques etc
Matter concepts require characteristics
Mother's spoken words visually transition personal individual
    speeches orientated
Educated tests are an admission to
Dependency of whitefella interviews
Educate quantitative human based degrees must give greater
    technological importance
To aborigines arts workforces
Verbal bull forms activity to this stage
Verbal bull dust relates modern graduates
Our age video cds and tapes are cramming
Children's aspired relevant solving
Our old memory social reality are utility to recipes imperative
    inherent to levels
Foundation only develops by black jarjum's
Handling problem-solving
Listening in rich atmospheres and giving back respective
    points within learning

Lionel Fogarty

Mingom Treatment If Possible

Your morning cry made me want to die
I like to die with the water hen
with the turtle the porpoises
The fish; even the porcupines
I like to dead with the kangaroo emu snakes and opossums
I like to dead with the goanna birds and seagulls butterfish
    even pelicans
koalas; eaglehawks
I like to dead with all nature's brothers and sisters
I love to die with my body in the boughs up high in a tree
I love my bones to be dried out then put in cave;
I love to die wrapped in bark
About six or three feet deep dug out then the logs put by sides
    and branches to make a platform then
put the bark over me and fill in my body with earth
I love to die with singing; dancing and crying around my grave
I like to hear while I'm laying dead the political cultural
    speakers and fires all night till dawn
I love to die with my aboriginal freedom colours all around me
I love to have a funeral with live music played by yidaki
    (didjeridoo)
even a song by our great singer protest cultural singing
I love all my murri people
to come to my funeral;
I don't want one miggloo there
I love to die and live on in
Dreaming I came from
I love to die and be buried in
any murri land

Lionel Fogarty

Mortal to Immortal

The morning spits up the sun
Below my bed my lips peel
Yo our childs Hullabaloo over
Keeping our first abo culture good
Clean shaven back lands
And we sunstruck by a colourless talk by Americanos
The afternoon spits up the starred night
Below my head lay eyes looking
At the noses arse-end of this world
A first fella said I want to be oblivious
'What for?' cos midday squinting toward
A trespassive on murri land
Rumour field the house of every
Peoples spirits of: 'How come a sickle moon kisses earth and
    found out what heart'
Toned cry sitting love makes
So fuck love for yesterdays dump
So lullaby away dreams that don't come true
Those murri skills remain are
Future clumsy flinch with business
Those murri hobnailed on naming
Each other cabs calm in drawer for a bit of money
The rituals gentle murri sorcery
Gives ancient weathered faces
Stout to taut the looter?

Awake now readers and seed basic
Eternal life humble shipped out
Of man's sorrow affairs
Murri old commanded us us
Murri young commanded us us
The morning wings me to supreme sacrifice
According to the perished

Lionel Fogarty

Salt

He steps out onto the dry, white lakebed.
Hears the crunch of crystals underfoot.
Tries not to imagine whiteness creeping
over rubber and dusting leather on its
journey to his ankle. He keeps his feet
moving all the same. He understands the science:
the shallow root systems of introduced plants,
the water that rises from deep underground,
bringing with it things that are best kept buried.
He invokes the mantra of electron transfer,
of ionic bonds that form when water evaporates.
Magnesium sulfate. Calcium sulfate. Sodium chloride.
He knows the physics and the chemistry of it all,
but when he bends down on one knee and takes
a pinch between his thumb and fingers, feels the
grains' sharp edges intent on piercing skin,
he knows it isn't salt he's standing on.
It's the powdered glass they put into the flour.

Adam Ford

The Sparrow

I.
Night spheres through
the window frame,
it weeps and calls
me to its edges.

Tin snipped streetlights
dagger elbows splinters.
I peer out

and take my eyes
to its borders.

Face by face I forgot
all our rules.

II.
Green metal dust
spirals up damply
from the glint in the road.

Wollongong has collected
the day's rust –
fed into the mouths of dogbone.

Another white arrowed stone
rolls along the window ledge,
aims into town,

where Crown St designs
memory sounds. Vagrant voices
entwine the streets.

III.
Three weeks removed
the bubble
of your paint fumes.

Its grunge runs
and the moon pulls
east. Salaat drops

pinching fingertips.
We raptured together
away

from sand tongues
and I threw back a thousand
plastic stars.

IV.
I wait and outpour
a cigarette into a temperamental tilt,
tips lift off
clipping
the framed ledge.

My sheets grow into
your shell, while our words
replicate in the walls.

V.
Streetlight sweeps and coils
behind my eyes. It hemispheres
across the tilt of Town.

I screw a cigarette
into window brick,
step back, turn off
the kitchen light
and stare at what you left.

VI.
Twelve yellow sparrows
emerge from the window frame.
You gratified in a

myriad of flaps. Birds that dart up
along brick,
collecting the kitchen light

tossing it around,
taking it with them

into the back of the wall
where yellow saturates
an inky tag.

I saw you drain electric
when you grew them
from fingertips.

Its us, you said.

VII.
Oily seeds sat
underneath my skin.

Muscle straw weaved
over my arms, rippled
against my breast bone.

The golden iron blaze
bloomed
across my chest.

I swelled.

VIII.
I got a tattoo,
I said to you once.
A sparrow.

Shave. Grow a
weapon. But you left
to spray lines into walls.

The flame
developed macules across
the cleft of my neck.

Weedy muscles grew –
twitching slick.
Untouchable.

Only the murmur of bricks
said you'd left
after I broke you purpuric.

IX.
The swallow
turned razor sharp,
it slip-slided
through my limbs.

It hid inside my rib cage
and nested.

My knees spread blue.
I fell north
in my sleep.

X.
Spray cans sit
beside the window,
gulping down dust of months
and moths drop
clutching wings.

I'll run like bubblegum and combust
geometric: fluoro pink like blue.
You liked being in a club of blondes.

XI.
Wollongong train station
makes me a decoy.
The ticket machine ebbs
a flock of coins.

Elderly women scrunch
white napkins
in and out of a flora form.

XII.
Across the platform passengers
clip past a train line map,
tangled in graffiti lines.

Twisted
track routes tagged
in your rail web.

You once told me to search
for the place
where trains grow knots

in the rails. You said it's where you hide
and wait to strike, to
wrap it in your golden paint cocoon.

I stand in front
of your sprayed lines
spread across
the train route map

and my eyes idle on its edges,
looking for a way in.

Adam Formosa

Morning Light

… morning light entering by way of a mouth, you turn

Our bodies: the voices of shadows, unstable but nowhere bright,
as near enough … this long moment changed gorgeously
and now differently costumed. Whole imagined cities
still hover overhead to overlay, in ever-tightening lines,
their well-made feet or walls of reason. Insanity reflected
so that only now it can approach the *condition* of music.
Its materials and architecture wait somewhere singing …
buried in each other's bodies

Here is your opening: pulse, breath

It is Summer
Insects beat their fragile wings against glass
and from the sky, your mouth smiles, cities disappear
and look … it is the unclothed morning light that enters.

Angela Gardner

infallibility

writing face down
the only sense is collage

praying for approval in front of a statue
godmother telling mother to tell you off for idolatry

the minute you answer back you are being subversive

leave me alone on the page
I can feel the capillaries breaking in my legs
and my pen running out of ink

I am up to my knees in the story of:
we are only doing this because we love you

slashing tyres
cutting poems

when beliefs are more important than people
we are beetles on our backs

children in strollers holding dolls on nooses

prostitution doesn't stop rape
a child holding a bunch of daisies bigger than her face
it exists because of rape

footsteps in the cemetery
I will dye my hair in Autumn
control being a response to loss

a belief you can't be wrong
a belief you can't control your urges

both beliefs that you can't
and here in the story up to my hips

Claire Gaskin

Earshot

Basking within the inner circle
this language approached you
from all directions, with caresses

& gestures in the genial air, an earworm
burrowing into a brain sparking
& elastic with connection. Its ornaments

could be the servants of melody, but
it becomes evasive, whispering just
out of earshot & retreating indignantly

when you reach to clutch at some words
held in the red lotus-seed-shaped jars
with small mouths, to cradle a phrase

at the perfect moment: the foreign tongue
spurning each overture & spitting back
uncountable nouns like rice & water

Jane Gibian

A Forest:

Come closer and see / see into the trees / find the girl / while you can
—The Cure

Winter came today, *into the trees*. Caught out, like a hibernation
misstep, you reach for the superfine merino. The fog blanketing
out the valley like an antiquated smoke machine and the old
British tourists in their tweed jackets suddenly looking right
at home super-imposed on the mulchy trails, where a day ago
English women were exposing their chicken arms. What sort of
poet are you anyway? V.V. came here for the cheap heroin and
you haven't so much as chewed paan. The ladies of the lyric are
winning all the awards and Melbourne is a UNESCO city of lit.
The bio-diversity is all in your iTunes library, as you sit cross-
legged on the bed drinking tea, the apple glowing like an orb.
Aman brings you supper and a hot water bottle. Why not put
Nick Drake on and be done with it? Or is this more a Murakami
moment? Your particular ability is to attenuate, so listening
becomes a kind of ultrasound. The fog *is* the imaging medium.
Perhaps things are more transparent than you thought, the past
is definitely a deeper contemplation. Why should any of these
things be co-opted by the other side? It's not too hard to adjust
your meter, to leave space for the translation, your command of
the colloquial carrying all the necessary Trojans.

Keri Glastonbury

Hey Hemingway!:

Mysore, India

Yes, The Sun Also Rises (if not the emasculated).
The romantic ennui of a Mills & Boon for men, as Brett
sidles up to the bar in her fedora.

We like boy's names for girls too.

The paperback was lying around the guest house.
Another tiny locus for a giant movement.

I thought Flora and Marie, the new proprietors,
were French lesbians. Last night I saw them on their scooter
pulling up to a restaurant, as I walked past in my black raincoat.

I forget I blend in with the bitumen.

I know a G. Stein too and our conversations also
coined something lost.

We're all hooked on sun salutes here.

Keri Glastonbury

Hotel Hyperion

I. The history of space travel

In truth, the history of space travel
is a history of rooms.
　　　　　— I kept a room
those eleven years in the Hotel Hyperion.
It had been a prison, the first in orbit,
and its guest rooms kept the old locks.
The Futures Museum was paying me
for artefacts from the failed outposts
of settlement. Those years, voyaging
to the forsaken places, I slept
more than I woke, never shaking off
the after-weight of anaesthetic sleep
before I slept again, places that held then
in my mind like so many self-lit
dreams, but for the relics I brought back.
　　　　　— I used to time my waking
for the radio line where their abandoned
voices first shaped words in static
the way a figure wades out of mirage
dripping with light. Whispers, pleas,
accusations, prayers: voices in their afterlife
talking me out of sleep ...

II. Deserted settlement, Titan

This glassed-in world the scale of memory, self-
            possessing its own loss. Here,
        never the small slant rain that is intimate
            because it does not know you.
Only a path beneath a trellis weighed with vines
            by fruit trees under lights,
        the bright fruit set in many-shadowed leaves –
    Structure of vaults that holds in air, its whirr
            of engines subdued to a sound
    of bees eating out their palaces in fallen fruit,
            crop on crop, seasons built
        into the lights, and here the bright fish turn
            as if by clockwork
    in a clear-walled stream – It is so orderly and
    strange, a sort of camera obscura that would
            teach how to make
        the illusion of depth on paper, which is to say
            They lived their whole lives
            here. I am collecting things as they were
            in somebody else's dream,
trading in years for them as though the dream were mine.

III. Discovery

Routine search, Kuiper Peninsula.
This blank of Titan where the wind is
visible, anodised with cold –
               I don't hear it.
I am closed in my life, my machine-
fed breath, a true ghost haunting
the loneliest idea –
               these footprints out
from the settlement's small world of
manufactured atmosphere. Strange to see
and not to feel the cold –
               this ice-waste eating
glacier-like rifts into itself, fit to the screen
as if to say I have walked through mirrors,
shrinking to scale
               self-lit worlds –
Then, like pure fiction, their ship,
propped in debris, years lost to a trick of light.
White burn of standby engines
               and an airlock door
to where they are, still held in quiet:

unfinished children, in their Perspex
coffers, hermetically sealed
          the clear infusion.
drip-feeding still an unbroken knowledge
of dreams. Only, like some more precise
hallucination, on their ice-
          backed skin this
filigree of ice. The machine is breathing them
miniature gardens of abjured existence, resembling
the mechanism of a clock
          copied in snow.

Lisa Gorton

The Humanity of Abstract Painting

for Diena Georgetti

I.
Afternoon rain on the windows,
bare rooms stilled with light – an idea of the house
that had always haunted your life in it,
as if to say This is the machine of the present.
It reinvents experience as a daydream.
This is the empty house –

II.
The rain sound is less like sound
than it is the trick of familiar places, which return
things to the conditions of imagery.
Boxes filled with what you own. Now
room after room you make this more entire
architecture of memory –

III.
An infinite of loss closed
in its frame like the house of a modernist: furniture
fit to the room. Everything thought, every
thing remembered, as if somebody else's
house now has you in it, a collector of things as they were
in somebody else's dream –

IV.
Because a collector is free
as facing mirrors prove the renewal in what it is
to be possessed. Rooms you could walk through
blind, windows of rain-coloured light.
This is the house that silence returns to you.
This is the empty house.

Lisa Gorton

Sanssouci

Frederick the Great's
summer palace, a rococo-style
pavilion, with windows
that could make
a glass house,
is the yellow
of Hollandaise sauce
and has egg-white detail.

It arises, encrusted with sculptural
gestures, on a billow
at the edge of a great park. Below
the blazing gravel
of its forecourt, there is laid out
what has been the project
of his heirs, also –

the gardens. These are loose,
English, pluralist,
and proliferate
among copse and alcove,
gathering mist
in any niche or hollow
toward dusk. They've
shaggy hedges and rank-
looking northern trees
by Cranach,
are not at all Platonist.

Frederick came here
if he wished to be alone,
with just a hundred servants,
and played the flute, in thigh boots,
before banks of candlelight,
or walked the grounds with Voltaire.
He gave shelter, from Catholic
and Protestant, to La Mettrie,
who had pointed out
man is a machine of meat
driven by appetite
(there was a comparison made also
with a plant) – i.e.,
we are subject
to cause and effect.
Frederick delivered his eulogy.

The Prince liked homosexual jokes
and saw his wife once a year
at a state occasion.
His nephew was his heir.
He wrote an 'Anti-Machiavel'
and had four horses shot
from under him in battle.
He was a hero to Napoleon.

Although a *philosophe*
he built an army
of those who had no say
and took them
into hand-to-hand slaughter,
to break upon his hip
the sway
of Austria-Hungary.
As Engels used to quip,
History fulfils her purposes –
her potential – by wading
over stacks of corpses.

The clear-eyed Greeks
were in Frederick's thoughts
at Sanssouci,
as seen by the statuary
he'd planted
at each of the circuses
along the main gravelled courses
and in alcoves
off the mazed pathways.
(At major junctions, as well,
there are fountains, each a simple
pool, with its tall
water like an ostrich feather.)

The gods and heroes here
are shown
at what they've always done,
which is bestir
trouble. Life
as the Greeks knew
is mischief. To interfere
is the way of Nature.
Aphrodite, though
she turns her face away
and covers breast
and pubis, is inflammatory
just because
of her modesty.
Beside her are displayed,
along with a wheelbarrow and spade,
the usual abductions, rapes
and punishments,
in radiant nudity.

In one arbour
Hercules crumbles the spine
of Antaeus, who is embraced
about the waist, and hung
off the ground, a leg thrown
back, a toe feebly
reaching, to plug in
to the Earth.
Cinch of his girth
by half, his swollen scream
soundless, the extruded tongue
like a spear thrust
from behind, out of his mouth.
Undermined, the whole building
Is coming down.

For those sauntering
of a late afternoon, the trees
and shrubberies
make a backdrop
to this scene, and are laden
with leaves, as a window
with blown rain. You see,
drawn near, in the level
glare, that foliage
is like tongues,
and how it is these which the sun
lays its wafer upon.

Robert Gray

About Bats

The bats which got in
last night
through the broken extractor fan
upstairs
while we were talking
on the phone

tiny micro-bats
with pale chests and
black-brown wings three times their pygmy-shrew
body size: they touch surfaces
in soft, velvet splatters,
they land like dusters,
they're softness (a word hard to stomach in poems),
they make the air flutter when they swerve around,
their speed so fine they look like dark flames
evaporating in mid-space –

well, the bats
were that 'soft' surprise moment –
at first I'd thought one of them
then thought two,
letting one out of the window –
really, there'd been three –
whirling in mid-air like shape-shifters
or like genii
like magic hands
in the electric lamplight

that breeze flittering round me
caused by bats, let's call it zephyr
(French ones are 'bald mice')
let's call them 'gentle-breeze mice'
as the Chinese might do
acknowledging
the way their webbed paws
'wings'
give a huge circling embrace
to a small part of the world,
fitting in through frequency

guessing contours
sheering away and around
without sight   alert through the whole
system to the looming bulk tanker
twenty storeys tall on the long dark swollen Pacific Ocean
(the refrigerator near the door)
or the fine filigree of currents
(my pedestal fan) in their flight's veer
and dart

objects being sensed in their richness
along every fibre,
in every nerve as possible harshness,
as passage and entry,
as cloths and clouds through the muscle
held forever
as a branch of apple flowers blossoming –
on the edge –
in the river of movements where
air and water meet constantly
a river of sun-flashes sensitised like a dancer's
placing of a physical counterpoint on a rhythm:

bats being themselves makers of shape and shaping
shapers of a purely undefinable intuitive shape
not unlike a gesture of
pure thoughtless good intent
in which each creature
(in mind or urge, it's the same)
(heard or overheard, there's no difference)
changes into the volume and shift
of things fingered out between
thought and love and flesh

:small black bats circling and
soaring in the kitchen at night

Martin Harrison

Aubade

If an extremely blue, misty, angular winter early morning
leaving its traces, its minnows and shimmers, in your eyes,
almost creating blindness in the night's dew-spattered end
and certainly patching up those palm-tree tops with trains of
    rain clouds,

if the man on the beach, the millionaire Russian dog galloping
    by him,
if the tourist's dropped coin swept up from the sand's scallops
and the wind-touched oleander leaves clicking like strips in a
    flyscreen –
if all these would suddenly make sense (in a burst of light)

(in the white outflow of a breaking wave) (in a quick overjoyed
memory of you) then I would see exposed all the future:
I'd be someone standing in a farm on a stony mountain side,
looking out to a valley of mown fields. I'd be in a fifth-floor
    Paris apartment

looking down at the boulevard's brackish traffic. I'd know
    where I was,
I'd know how I am. All this is how the sun reveals your beauty,
and my own immersion in it, all my speechless delight:
the minnows, the shimmers, that bright and rapid shade,

have now become my innerness, my inner sense of you.
Down the shore, misty blue withdraws from a daybreak sea.
I cannot live without you, cannot accept more emptiness.
I've woken up with you after the whole night was dark with fire.

Martin Harrison

Eurydice

Slow lordly clouds,
A fine-spun summer day,
And over-ripe, dark smells
Of grass in seed,

You coming through
Our kitchen door, white dress
Ironed by the sun,
Your collarbones

Barely hiding,
With lips apart
As if to taste the morning air
Alive with light,

Your eyes
Caressing mine,
Hair over cheekbones, blown
Across your mouth,

Those noble clouds
Aloof, yet knowing then
What door
You pass through now.

Kevin Hart

The Museum of Shadows

You'll find it in the dingy part of town.
Its thermostat is always set way low
To limit time that's spent with all that dark.
Old folk are quickly weeded from the line.

Umbrologists have glowing labs inside,
Machines that catch rare shadows from the past:
The shadow of an angel's trembling wing
While waiting for the Virgin's yes or no;

And there's a Hall of Oddball Shadows, too:
Renaissance Lords who had their shadows sit
Late afternoons while lazing back with wine.
Their portraits swagger over ten feet tall.

Go see a silhouette of Gengis Khan
Or Vlad bent over, working on a spike,
A Japanese at home inside a wall,
Go see young Cleopatra's nose, or else

The Hall of Modern Shadows, nearly done:
Curators go from door to door with knives
That cut a shadow free. My worthy friend,
Soon you may feel a cold blade at your heel.

Kevin Hart

Still Water

the dawn a cup of dust
kids yelling like grown-ups

the car works
the neighbour's dog barks all night

years passing too fast
to see the trees slowly fall

his eyes like the faraway ocean
her mouth like a shut purse

their loving
like trying to save breaths

whole towns turning brown
the branches that won't bend

Matt Hetherington

Gannets

They departed, the gods, on the day of the strange tide.
—JOHN BANVILLE, The Sea

Of a gannet I could say –
like Ian Thorpe on the blocks
like a Porsche outside the club.

Sheer finesse is the thing.
But the gannet is more serious than that.
It is grave presence.

Gannets gives off ceremony.
As a congregation
they exude license.

I know, I live almost
as near to them
as I must to myself.

They propagate at Pope's Eye
just out in the bay: too far to swim –
approachable by small boat.

From a distance, the rookery is a scrum of white
all frisky innocence, like a flock of nuns
their habits dove-toned, crossing St Peter's Square.

Closer in, you get the foul whiff of rocks.
Bobbing within a stone's throw of the mess
the gannets hit you with the force

of a battalion of defrocked priests
bodies snow-white, their nakedness gross –
powers stripped of merit, all terribly free.

Gannets strut, they preen – 'We are still the best.'
If they have a God it's put extra time into the arrowhead
beak or spear tip: a streamlined weapon that owns the head.

The eye is bevelled in black stripes to the beak.
Flat caps soften us up with pale mustard –
yellow hinting at ravenous.

The mystery is, the closer you look at the single-pointed
hungry ones, the more they seem identical –
an aspect of swarm, like lice.

Their grades of white save them, give pleasure
to the eye like a nautilus shell
like marble, like a stick of clean chalk.

And their flight, their flight when they take off
straight up, each bird is pure unto itself, like nothing else.
High in the heavens, it is a monastery of one.

The arrow becomes a kite
as one hangs, hawkish over the South Channel.
It's deep out there.

The sea is mackerel.
The penitent is homicidal.
The plummet is what it's made for

its white power marvellous with death.
If you're sitting in a safe boat
a resurrection looks credible:

the gannet reappears in the chop.
For an instant, a hopelessly heavy shag –
then soaring to do beautiful damage again.

Barry Hill

Plum Juice

Without knowing
　　　I turned the page
　　　　　with wet fingers
on my new copy
　　　of Du Fu –
　　　　　smearing 'The Sick Horse'.

And later
　　　when I thought them dry
　　　　　I came to 'Facing the Snow'
the pictures he painted –
　　　skin cracked
　　　　　with pure lament:

　　　Above the battlefield
many new ghosts are crying;
　　　steeped in sorrow
a lone old man is chanting.

　　　The ladle lies useless
the wine jar toppled over;
　　　the stove grows cold,
red embers slowly fading ...

And still my touch was dark –
      a purply red,
            an indelible ink:
my brush is swollen
      to write the end
            of our running wars.

*No news comes
from anywhere this winter.
In empty air
a sad old man is writing.*

Barry Hill

Primavera: The Graces

We know when the wind bends down
to tangle the raw silk and the oranges
thicken their perfume that our natures
are dark after all. No time for angels now.
It is spring. Death is in the trees,
in the petals shining underfoot like glass.
Let the dance quicken in the blood,
let it shake the speared buds down
like hail, let it hollow the minds of men
and bring them to us, howling like dogs.
See, we move through the black wood
like gods through time, turning and turning
as if it is all reversible: the light sieving
through the branches, the wet grass
arching up to our touch, the pale seeds
and their red and white unpeeling.
The end is in the beginning, it is our song.
The men will come, rough mouths agape
at the crabbing of light and shadow
at our feet – we have no stake in it.
Our art is too long; the circle
will not break. Only the birds hurtling
through the air like flung stones
know the truth: it is in the tiny fandango
of their pulse, in the leaves scratching
them through the air, in their descent
which is short and unspectacular
and spills out of them like wine.
Fear it: your lives are short too.

Sarah Holland-Batt

The Macaw

Blue is not the colour of paradise.
See the macaw sommersault out into a sea

of air, a fork of cracked blue lightning
jagging down the brainless sky,

a rudderless blade. With palette knife
wings, he ekes and scrapes the day's

bottled colour, and lives in air, is air.
Do not call him vacant: he has intent,

though his face is empty, he buffets, a splay
and flash of navy scraps, a brush

of dripping indigo, and stages
a surprise assault on the poor slovenly

trees, the tropic fruit. All entropy,
that knickknack beak. He shakes down

a rain of blood-berries, a rich drench,
and feeds. Chatter is as chatter does:

his ear turns transistor for scratched stone
and rust. Flight calls him, always,

over the one-upmanship of the canopy,
its smug creepers strangling the weak

like fat snakes, that sad hierarchy.
Above it all the macaw blazes, guerrilla

sky-mimic flickering along the horizon's nerve,
mad with his blueness, an oceanic

reliquary, deep Cousteau ultramarine
that inverts sky and sea, full bolt blue,

and the sun stings with him. From his view
the Andes are dust, pallid cousins of the Alps,

and the gold-bulbed ants who squall
and clamber in the mud glitter

meaningless as jewels. He fossicks
anxiously through spring's sudden greens,

that rush, and each poisonous seed
festers in his gut, heavy as history.

Morning, he sings the bullet out of it,
a dark star dyed almost invisible

against day's amnesiac backdrop.
The seasons repeat. The macaw forgets

nothing; he hoards it all like ambergris.
Palms fray in the wind, fronds drop

ratty showers of budded fringe,
swathes of forest and petty tyrants

shrink. Everything moves into the eye
of the macaw, native and comprehending,

everything sinks into that black bowl.

Sarah Holland-Batt

Darwin's Taxidermist

A Negro lived in Edinburgh and gained
his livelihood by stuffing birds,
which he did excellently,
and taught me

when a thing is killed the mouth
should be opened, cleaned as if your own,
filled with cotton
and any wounds the same.

Without an audience or food a mouth
is just a wound he said while labelling jars
POISON   DRIED MOSS
GLASS EYES   SWEET HAY.

Lie the animal on its back, quiet legs
pushed aside, take the scalpel in the right
and with the left separate the hair
like a loving groom.

Work in a straight line to better God
he laughed. Be firm:
why should the skin loosen its hold at all easily?
Turn back the skin on either side

and a wild red land is revealed.
Take much care in setting the eyelid;
the expression – of belief, nonbelief –
depends altogether on this.

L.K. Holt

Lyrebird

Ned Kelly as landscape – Sid Nolan's idea

         Ned Kelly member

 of the family

Ned Kelly as bully

          Ned Kelly softy

keeper of paycocks. Ned Kelly as ploughshare

       Rosella can of condensed

Ned Kelly as the auld Surfer's Paradise

      of lagoons and shrikes

        Ned Kelly as a green Ribbon –

 twenty years in yr.

         pocket

Ned Kelly as Red Kelly in drag

 If you believe Peter Carey

Ned Kelly as the October mow –

              & old scotch

 foreskin jokes

       Ned Kelly as lunatic fringe of desert

 spring, as Meaghan Morris

      Leaving Tenterfield in her teens, or

 Newcastle forever

Ned Kelly as bushel of Tasmanian heads

Ned Kelly as a Mentone bookie in suede

      Fletcher Jones Jeans. Ned Kelly as Melton

 junkie. Ned Kelly as Bon Scott's

Letters to Adelaide & sister

      Irene

Ned Kelly is a TV celebrity'
s dog wading the scum at St Kilda sniffing
    at the golden band of freeway
         i' th' West
Ned Kelly as downtown Melbourne shamrockery
:conspiracy of clover, *'trefoil'*, or when you're German
        Dreiblattbogen
'De Tird Oiye' say Dubliners, meaning pagan punch
Ned Kelly as the night-jar, bone-jar
 little jar of bones we'd worship if
  we c'ld find it if
    we c'ld find it.

Duncan Hose

Anne Frank's Sister Falls from Her Bunk

Bergen-Belsen, 1945

From the well of my bunk,
I watch you fall. You do not stir
when I call or scratch at the lice that infect us all.
The cold-booted guard gives you a little kick.
A dirge plays on my frozen lips.
Water and dark earth, to which we return;
that's what you sound like, dragged from the room.

Three days pass without you here.
The typhus unfurls its crimson flowers.
I try to speak but find I have no mouth.
I'm a black dog, muzzled.
To say 'heart' is unheard of.

Each night I climb a few more rungs
up the ladder out of myself,
into the attic where we hid once, quiet as bones.
The sky is improbably blue.
I am rising like smoke towards you.

Lisa Jacobson

Perianthetical Apple, Cherry, Plum

Tree petticoats, false lingerie, winged flotsam,
fall to me, sift and shake, and bus the breeze,

lay petalline on beds of gardens, float pink
and white from cherry trees, collect, dispel,

disperse, deceive, stay on, lie down;
maybe your fall perturbs me?

Set out in fives and threes, your pose
as clustered perianth is disposed by puffery.

Be flower wrap, pollen pot, carpel king,
tepal tide, bee bait and wasp impersonator,

house of plum state, modified leaf palace that duples
into picnics, prints, pillow words and porcelain,

sometimes cover of stigma, style and anther,
for *Malus domestica, Prunus serrula, Prunus mume,*

you are glory, gobsmack, gregal, descending grace-note
and colour grid, giddy girasole that bends sunlight,

an acrobat of gravity and air, a blow-in,
you blouse, a disrobing beauty queen
and everything between, play petal mist for me.

Carol Jenkins

Alfred Wallace's Dragons

Flores, Indonesia

Komodo dragons perch high on their remnant turf
too heavy and too young for this time
for our fast sick air
Still their milky eyes shutter and wind on
like old press cameras retrieved
but lacking sound
What the dragons remember most is the sound of pencil
scratching out the shape of worlds
in the mandelbrot detail of a lizard's frill
This was colonial finders keepers:
the rush to trace the prehistoric gaze
blood-let nibs dipped in adrenal ink
Still, the same incoherent mountains shoot up
from rheumatic sea floors
restless to begin again
knowing how to goad flat-earthers and surveyors
to rheumy-eyed phantasms of possession
Even the crater lakes were coloured red, green and aqua
– a child's codeless vision
He was racked with fever then
empires of throat and wrist
pinned by grubby lace
In the morning cool he stepped out one last time
dragons manufacturing
antediluvian poisons in the shade
Who could hope to comprehend a mountain
dressed in two kinds of shot green?

He thought of his jilted fiancée
her love of hued cloth
love as antivenom
for the bite of excess truth
It was then the side-eyed creatures knew
they need not learn to talk
That he had seen two sorts of nature
(stateless tropic and subtropic)
clinging to either side of the mountain
and would let them be.

A. Frances Johnson

Alfred Russell Wallace (1823–1913) was a British naturalist, explorer, geographer, anthropologist and biologist. He is best known for independently proposing a theory of evolution due to natural selection that prompted Charles Darwin to publish his own theory. His interest in biogeography resulted in his being one of the first prominent scientists to raise concerns over the environmental impact of human activity.

This Is Not Dove Cottage

The house is talking dirty, it's that time of night
when heat goes off the naked ceiling,
& closer & closer, step by step,
wood gets hold of the plaster,

& it's better to be with you in Sydney.
My books, sure, are large with lakes & grandeur,
tramping the vale's good for thinking,
but the heat of your arm is more than thought.

I wish the house would smile,
I wish Wordsworth had
had a sense of humour, or stayed with his
French *maîtresse*, what was her name – *Annette* –

we could talk then, take our time, lakes are
far from here & air fills with
irregular ticks, you are far from here,
the house fills with dirty noisy cold, somewhere

there's a joke in this that never made it back
into revolution, *bon hiver* is
stretching the point,
what is your hand doing over there?

Jill Jones

Grey Shrike-thrush

for Oliver Gasperini

'Ah, so this is the answer. But what is the question?'
—Gertrude Stein's dying words

Flute voices of the thrushes ripple and trill
so that a question's shaped in every tune,
silver enquiries falling from each bill,
as though all truth resided in their tone.

But what the questions are we cannot know.
Victorians claimed that they were lovers' pleas.
Our century goes for territorial show
and martial challenges blown through the trees.

Yet to each song the answer is the same;
the phrase comes back exactly as it went.
Each note burns brightly with its own wild flame;
the answer echoes fervour and intent.

So all the day, in shadow and in sun,
question and answer still resound as one.

Frank Kellaway

Faultlines

We're still awake but night's descended
I am feeling in the wrong
The uneasy silence should have ended
But I have listened far too long
It's my fault because I've tended
As always, just to go along
The uneasy silence should have ended
But I have listened far too long

Your fears, which I have apprehended
I have lived in shame among
It's my fault because I've tended
As always, just to go along
Your fears, which I have apprehended
I have lived in shame among

The world feels sad and undefended
I feel weak: I should feel strong
It's my fault because I've tended
As always, just to go along
The world feels sad and undefended
I feel weak: I should feel strong
What's not a fence cannot be mended
With a silent useless tongue
It's my fault because I've tended
As always, just to go along

Peter Kenneally

In My Wheat-Bag Hood

For the rain my uncle throws me a wheat-bag hood
in the long home paddock of the past.
My shoulders will stay dry. I trudge through mist and touch a
forest.
Jute rasps my brow.
In my wheat-bag hood I hear tomorrow. No radio chips in.
I eat old men's crusted wisdom. They strip the bark from trees.
Brahms overwhelms me.

The city pales against my wheat-bag hood.
Someone shoves me my first drink.
But still I'm dry. I sometimes guess what's coming.
After the do at the footy club she'll get laid I know
and will not like it.

It's steady trudging. Rain plucks at the taint of jute. It makes
for honesty.
My cousin dies against white sheets. Again there's Brahms.
I span Australia in my wheat-bag hood.
Kosciuszko's not so big. The Mallee's just one step.
I hear boots on boards. I wait for moonrise
to snag in pepper-trees. We sleep in the truck
in the silo queue.

I chew guilt like cud in my wheat-bag hood.
There's no pretending, so I knock.
The door stares. I knock again.
I walk back past yesterday. My mother considers
the bull's huge sway and laughs.
I smell damp candour in my wheat-bag hood.
My shoulders even now aren't wet. The jute abrades my brow.
Suddenly I've never had children. And here's the door.
I knock. The door still stares.

Graeme Kinross-Smith

Goat

Goat gone feral comes in where the fence is open
comes in and makes hay and nips the tree seedlings
and climbs the granite and bleats, through its line-
through-the-bubble-of-a-spirit-level eyes it tracks
our progress and bleats again. Its Boer heritage
is scripted in its brown head, floppy basset-hound ears,
and wind-tunnelled horns, curved back for swiftness.
Boer goats merged prosaically into the feral population
to increase carcass quality. To make wild meat. Purity
cult of culling made vastly more profitable. It's a narrative.
Goat has one hoof missing – just a stump where it kicks
and scratches its chin, back left leg hobbling, counter-
balanced on rocks. Clots of hair hang like extra legs
off its flanks. It is beast to those who'd make devil
out of it, conjure it as Pan in the frolicking growth
of the rural, an easer of their psyches when drink
and blood flow in their mouths. To us, it is *Goat*
who deserves to live and its 'wanton destruction'
the ranger cites as reason for shooting on sight
looks laughable as new houses go up, as dozers
push through the bush, as goats in their pens
bred for fibre and milk and meat nibble forage
down to the roots. Goat can live and we *don't know*
its whereabouts. It can live outside nationalist tropes.
Its hobble is powerful as it mounts the outcrop
and peers down the hill. Pathetic not to know
that it thinks as hard as we do, that it can loathe
and empathise. Goat tells me so. I am being literal.

It speaks to me and I am learning to hear it speak.
It knows where to find water when there's no water
to be found – it has learnt to read the land
in its own lifetime and will breed and pass its learning
on and on if it can. Goat comes down and watches
us over its shoulder, shits on the wall of the rainwater
    tank – our lifeline – and hobbles off
        to where it prays, where it makes art.

John Kinsella

Flight

Sometime in June or July, throw on a cable-stitched
grey jumper or even a thick coat for warmth,
take the afternoon off and head out past Kurnell
to Cape Solander. There, on the white sandstone cliffs
above the vast sprawl of the sea, look
for humpbacks heading north, swimming near the shore
to dodge the ocean current sliding south.
Witness, if you're lucky, a whale breaching –
the corrugated whiteness of its wobbly ascension,
the dark certainty and blazing glitter of its fall.
The cold breeze ruffles the diamond quilt
until it's as messy as an unmade bed, it tugs
at the waving tendrils of spear grass and at the tips
of your ears, it makes your eyes water
as if some old sadness has unexpectedly taken hold.
You can find no sign of a sea eagle, hovering;
you cannot name the endangered species
growing in this headland heath. But you can close
your eyes, you decide to do this simple thing,
electing to completely miss the whale if it rises again,
aware now of this immense, unknown life
going on around you, within you, as the buffeting,
lunging wind picks you up and gives you wings.

Andy Kissane

Horses

In Barcelona
she stood in a street twisted like smoke
listening to the sound of one hundred chocks of wood
coming down the granite mountain.
She smelt them before they reached her,
sweat on their flanks
hooves slapping the ground
hot yellow dust and
flies sipping the salt off chestnut skins
covered in bite marks and faded serial numbers.

When they rounded the corner
it was too late for her to do anything.
So she closed her eyes,
imagined she was a tree, a boat
anchored in the sea,
a lamppost.
She felt their breath,
warm whip of hair
strong as violin strings
as the wild horses
spilled around her like a bolt of velvet.

Old women wrapped
in the muted colours of mourning
stood in their doorways
amid the panicked chicken squall
unable to see anything but a walloping sheet of dust,
piss-warm rivulets
running down
their wrung-out tea-towel faces
listening to the sound of honky-tonk pianos,
this galloping band of horses.

Anna Krien

Travelling the Golden Highway, Thinking of Global Warming

Stringybarks in bloom;
a perfume like honey ice-cream.

Along the Prussian escarpment
two eagles work the updraft.

Cicada noise rises and falls
as if the mountain itself were breathing –

In panic.   Out relax.
In panic.   Out relax.

Manga pylons stride the valley,
millions of volts in their fists –

The car radio is plunged into static,
silver grids of capital/energy shift –

Open cuts. Artificial mesas –
Ulan coal warms the world.

Mike Ladd

The Finales

A Beethoven ending is not a true ending.

It can't be. There are no such things.

He raises the volume.

He tensions the strings and attacks ...

He draws silk across skin.

Still, God refuses to happen.

He pounds with that great club, his talent;
empurples the air
with the claim that a world has been won –

leaving his heirs
to *the doubts after Ludwig* –

who wanted so badly,
who travelled so close to their need:
Liszt, praying *technique*;
or Schumann, who thought that a deity
might be the yearning – the gulf – between keys.

None of them found what they looked for.

Where else to look then?

O how many died, in the wars,
that a story might end?

Martin Langford

Seeing Goats

You might encounter one in a dream
meaning fair weather, bountiful crops
or the welcome arrival of friends
from the margins of your life.

Sightings, while numerous, have never
been validated. Sheep in dreams
foretell an inability to protect yourself
while the appearance of a goatherd

and his belling entourage will soon
put that inability to the test.
Distance and blind faith can deceive
the serial reporter of sightings

and encounters – the spectral forms
of goats, winter-coated, their necks
and legs overlong, turned out to be
alpacas, standing sentry where a mob

of black-faced Border Leicester sheep
were feeding, oblivious to danger.
Reports of goats behind tall wire
levitating on a plain at Narromine

became a ragged parcel of deer, elevated
by heat lines, raw belief and dust.
Coleridge saw goats, as did Keats
and Marvell. Despite what literature

and film have to say, goats are not
tormented fiends with nowhere to rest –
they exist among us, avoiding exposure.
And for those who insist they've seen

a goat, it's more than likely a profound
persistent memory from a time
when fairytales and life were one
when fact and symbolism traded blood.

Midnight tours at penal colonies
offer flashlit, expert commentaries
on how, when graves were exhumed
in the name of genealogy or mistaken

identity, shapely heads and horns
were found beside the bones of men.
Make of this what you will. One goat seen
is another left to imagination.

Anthony Lawrence

The Decision

I studied the acceleration of subatomic particles.
    For weeks I lay awake
deconstructing aspects of the periodic table
    I believed were most
influential on the swing of moods, the molecular
    structure of the heart.
I used the words *postmodern* and *paradigm*
    with reckless abandon.
I went off the grid, going solar in my lifestyle
    and my head. I wept
for the floodlights rapeseed turns on, when
    flowering. I interrupted
myself with lengthy surges in the blood's trans-
    mission and direction.
I made amendments to my dreams, breaking
    the future down into
daily installments, wanting to be singular and real
    where previously
I'd been cultivating the style of other men.
    In theory I was capable
of love, in practice I was reading the Romantics
    and going to school
on the good marriages of friends. I focused
    on a time when people
toughed it out, knowing you'd find such self
    discipline irresistible.

Now I can't remember how I came to be without
    the need to prove
myself to you. Light and dark had not become
    epiphanies – it's just
that distance had unhinged the slow turnstile
    of my grief, and I
moved on, as they say, and while I hated losing touch
    with how I felt
when you had gone, given the chance to find you
    or lose myself again
in what it takes to make it through that kind
    of pain alive, I think
I'd hesitate, but not for long before the safety rail
    at the edge of my decision.

Anthony Lawrence

Lei Zu and the Discovery of Silk

from 'The Yellow Emperor Poems'

Was it a hand that released her sash
or the wind that swept it eastward?
It fell like a snake
landed like an arrow aimed at the river.

Did her gown open in its own time
or did the peaks of her breast-points swell
to breathful bounty, that all clothes
became impossible?

His fingertips, butterfly antennae,
lifting in plucked suspension
considered all surface options
testing the layers outside of thought.

On a leaf above, one worm
a winged cloud stuck in its throat
cocked its head, praised her behind its eye
yet the mystery of adoration
difficult for the air of its short life
returned to its patch.

It took four seasons of waiting
before the catkins' spores
quick-shot faster than a trilling flute note
to thicken the air, swirling
as if discharged by
the pulse-beat of bodies.

That day it was said
a ceremonious cocoon
fell into her teacup opening
to find her finger,
a billowing strand trailing
from a chrysanthemum sea
– a song for her emperor –
thread-written on blue sky

Like a night jar, I tremble in flight
follow a stream from Kunlun mountain
to the dark river's mouth
I ask the dawn hidden in reeds
to renounce honour
withhold its flame to keep you here.

What was the sun's collaboration?
Only the hearsay of doves
on a mulberry bough
doves that refused gossip,
yet Lei Zu stitched their beaks
on his battle coat
her visionary armour,
to madden
the four-headed stone-eating beast.

Michelle Leber

Rock Pool, Undertow Bay

*Charles Darwin studied barnacles for eight years before
completing his treatise* On the Origin of Species.

Bent over his galaxy, watercolour clouds
on breeze-rippled surface, plates opening
like snake eyes; where on his knees
faith became biological, a calcareous ministry
he longed to dissever, vivisection and its devotee.
To study *the swamping effect* – one way to survive
the salty breath of whelks that will grind holes
in those skeletons, to set him dreaming.
Did he admire their defiance, untroubled on
tide-swashed shore? Puzzled over

pantagruelian limbs – curious acts of genetic transfer?
Sirens of plankton in storm-weed latitudes
of an inquiring mind. Taught him to bathe with amoeba,
withstand displacement, the slap of whale tails.
Yet gutters and crannies of unknowing – twisting,
distorted, pounded by wind whorls and wave power.
And what he did understand taken by
the current then dumped on a foreign shore.
Smallest in vast expanse, perfect unfailing reminder
of everything unfathomable.

Michelle Leber

Conversations in a Family Van

I.
There was a pale green van.
I called it 'Bulk'
after the BLK in its number plate.
If cheap vinyl bench seats
purchased secondhand through the classifieds
could reassemble themselves and speak
(twenty years after their trip to the wrecking yard)
this is what they might repeat.

II.
Between marriages I'm driving
with my children aged two, three and five.
'We're having lunch with a lady.
She has two little daughters
called Nova and Buffy.'
'That's not their names.
No! You're tricking,'
small lungs angrily chorus.

III.
So each detail of my story is complete
for years I've been trying
to recall a name –
something to do with stars
but not Astrid.
A small grubby sedan
overtakes on my right,
the grimy chrome letters
on its boot spell the model name – NOVA
bursting on my mind
like a supernova.

IV.

My children aged eight, nine and eleven
are on the benches in the back,
their stepmother with me in the front.
We've picked them up
after a childbirth class.
'When that baby's born,'
the eight-year-old says,
darkening her voice like the witches in *Macbeth*,
'IT's not going to last long.
I'm making sure it's just Baby Bones.'

V.

Baby Bones is two years old,
strapped in a toddler's seat,
singing a meaningless song
to his sisters and brother as we drive.
At the end of his meaningless song
he loudly claps his own applause,
and his sisters and brother
laugh and clap too.

VI.

'Those glasses you're wearing are women's glasses,'
the young adults critique my spectacles
purchased from a hardware store.
They are oversize
and large gold medallions
decorate the frames.
'When I bought them I had no glasses on.
I couldn't see what they looked like.'

VII.
When the pale green van is young
I place my only child at the back
a baby girl
in a basket of white plastic wicker,
a tiny human being.
Driving down a busy highway
the rear door, not properly latched,
swings up of its own volition.
In the mirror I see a mass
of following traffic,
and the white basket,
poised at the back, as though about to fall out,
held only by its own small gravity.
I stop the van
and there's no conversation at all.

VIII.
The vinyl benches launch into direct speech,
the left and right sides of my brain speaking together:
'When he bought us secondhand
through the classified pages of the newspaper –'

The near bench:
'Another of his bargains –'

Both benches together again:
'His pale green van
was like an empty house,
just a driver's seat and passenger seat up front
like two little tombstones.
We furnished his van, we made it a home.
But what was the point of his van and us,
eight places for just two people?
There were no children then.'

The near bench:
'Another of his whims.'

The far bench:
'Perhaps they had children
to fill up the van and sit on us.'

IX.
The near bench:
'On the days he had the children,
picking them up from school
he was chronically late.
Always excuses.
A traffic pile-up. Or he'd run out of petrol.
They'd be standing on the footpath
almost in tears as he drove up.
He was a poseur, not a parent.'

The far bench:
'Remember that hot morning
his cheap reconditioned motor cracked in half.
The engine oil ebbed down the road like blood,
and we watched
the father and three little children
with their short fat legs
set out on the three miles to school.'

X.
The near bench:
'He'd drive for hours along mountain roads
to buy a blue or red rhododendron
with his last ten dollars,
and they'd start crying to go home.'

XI.
The far bench:
'Remember that time he filled the van
with banana palms
to plant along his front fence.
He threatened to call his house
"Banana Castle".'

The near bench:
'All because they were a bargain –
more than a fast-growing screen,
in eighteen months, a banana-palm jungle,
with fruit like shrivelled fingers
so he had to hack them all out –
a year of weekends with a mattock.'

The far bench:
'But spiders and fruit bats loved the big leaves
glinting in the streetlights at night.'

XII.
The near bench:
'He was young and stupid.
That marriage was a joke.
I'd see his hand reach out for hers
and she'd snatch her hand away.
Those banana palms were a big mistake.'

The far bench:
'Nothing is a joke.
I was the bench at the rear,
further away from children bringing up their milk,
the changing of nappies, the little quarrels.
I could watch the dawn
through the back window
grey clouds in the blue
that changed to burning pink.
What happened is what happened.'

Geoffrey Lehmann

Dress Circle

Melodramas are made for mothers.
The daughter thinks that one day
she'll graduate and take the lead.
Your right hand, little amanuensis,
eyeing off the competition.
Because I kept your secrets
I thought you were mine to keep.
Now I'm off the hook and at a loss.
Tra la la la la triangle
what'll I do without you?

Kate Lilley

Recalling the Bats

Borne of the air?
Do not believe it. They came
from the volcanoes:
Etna, Krakatoa, Pinatubo,
all those whose names
thrum at a frequency lower
than human bones.
But most of all, the nameless ones
before our time –
blown straight
up a surveying column of cloud.
From slow-pumping ash
dense as an underwater
roll of mud, they were flung:
hot cinders
cooling to charred bodies
which floated off
on clear currents. Far away
from the source, they populated
in dim canopies, between
boulders, the empty black
pitching of caves. Need evidence?

Take a live flying fox
wrapped in a towel or any cloth
thick enough to calm it,
and look into the eye: it is nothing
less than pure agate
glowing. Peer closer, you'll see
a million gold filaments
flexing like animated wood,
the pinhole pupil
a black pipeline travelling
endlessly into that
tiny boiling body. Lean over –
you'll smell acrid fumes,
the nostril-opening
ammonia rising
from orange-singed fur: you'll understand
why these creatures gorge
with such relentless clockwork
on rain-swollen
globes of fruit: it is an antidote
to the eternal
furnace of their lungs, the furious
clamping of their hearts.

Only night brings relief: an auditorium
                              of leaves
amplifying vocalisations
which mimic
the hot dry rub of flint stones
sparking into darkness. Only then
does air soothe
baked-leather wings which,
hung too long
in the naked sun,
become an efficient self-heating
apparatus of death.
So that the bats – remembering –
drag themselves
down trunks
    or drop from branches
one by one
where they lie: lumps of lava
cooling on the ground.

Debbie Lim

Attraction

between two houses, a bottle-o.
mapping like syrup or gravel
I've snuck between these two
houses fistfighting; plotting cats
in neighbourhoods of potential

> I've had so many non-Euclidean
> thoughts about you, noting the
> corruption of cricket (6s are renamed
> hi-maxis), the way cigs mark the
> pitch in corners exceeding one-eighty

in traffic, cars sublimate
stop and start like alchemy
white cockatoos skirt and pop,
lemonpippy. neighbourhood
cats are 'the smallest data'

> sex is topography (sketchy
> altitudes and effects of climate)
> Neopavlovian whatever, a Truffaut
> version, mapped like syrup or gravel
> into the hankie-pleats of time-sense

quilting is a tribute to angles
a worse idea than poetry. a woman
next to me sucks the room's air
through her teeth, asks, 'what do
you know about smoke signals?'

--

this digital version of English
mustard, pumpkinbread, sweetmeat.
sown pastures of barley wash into
gullies by yolk-cracking rain, losing
the raw materials of lunch

       we came right up to our throats
       with a fingernail's amount of rattly
       atoms buzzing, pointing to clouds
       and charging them each with new
       cloud-types, e.g. 'total fucking gas'

hologrammatic America, hi-def and
projected across the surface of
México. feral parsley seeding
on the median strip, angles flush with
lean-cut mince-meat, leathery chaps

       O, to fall in love! the first time
       you see two magnets drag clean
       a fishtank and deposit folds of
       algae onto the fingertip: a lesson
       on bloodflow digestion dejecta

archaeologies stack up and fast-
food together; pigeons squabble
for soy proteins. imagining that
everything can be translated as
'sex', I wait for some utterance

--

imagine the centre of a circle
is a moment of first collision.
we're here in a Lucretian poem
tied up in a basic scheme of
lambwool woodchop and milkskin

> where one cat appears and one
> disappears, an eccentric analogy
> about a wasp and indeterminate
> probability e.g. the pokies tech-gear
> insurance games and flight paths

ataraxia: pleasure of ingestion
ejaculation resistance tension
equilibrium. the rat-a-tat of energy
discharge. spreading is not just
difference but electronics, sonics

> A Dutch family is sweating uphill,
> crosshatching a steep headland south
> of Cronulla. from the sky, waves are
> constellations; sheep are modular units
> (bog silt chaff rainwater and milk)

inside every grass blade is a fat
lamb, suckled on milk and heat-
stroke – the sun's history jotted
on post-its, with the burn-out as
both beginning and ending

--

we are crosswording and feeling
that sex is just synonyms, a play
of equivalent others. pleasures in
difference are pleasures of emphasis:
the way an accent sits on a letter

      peaty-as-fuck scotch like a blood
      transfusion. I'm walking waist-
      high in a thistle farm glomming
      needle-thin encounters. percolate
      in this case is rain up through shoe

losing an apostrophe on a
Czech keyboard, I can no
longer contract or possess
so I begin to stretch out my
discourse, give it all away

      pleasure is emphasis, the one
      reiterated against or through
      the other. the difference between
      malting a milkshake and moulting
      a dog (the difference of smoke/mouth)

a play of equivalence; difference
is emphasis, Eros and errata, typo.
sediments of punchy stout or a rock-face.
all five were talking at once, one
couldn't see the irony re: Freddie Mercury

--

this is an event particle. site-specific
willy-willy, caravan relocated to
lagoon. a woman next to me sucks
the room's air through her teeth, says,
'Oh, look'

mapping a banjo solo, the strings move
toward each other like Muybridge's
horse. a turkey vulture flies in patterns
of forgetful desire, first here then
here then here (etc.)

American typologies: only
ever in Ohio or an mp3 Nashville,
the Atlantic ocean is dredged and
relocated for five bucks. a woman
sucks the air through her patois

things are being relocated, weathers
are cracking us open with genesis
narratives: tea leaf and harvest, toffee plates,
fish scales, cold sweats. when wool stinks
of Greek mutton Greek oil Greek nicotine

O kat, O puss kat, guard
me against moths against my
obsession with greeting cards,
against the threat of analysis and
the closed fur of downy circuitry

Astrid Lorange

The Petunias

I have believed enormously / have you?
—M.T.C. Cronin

To each and every flower that moment
of sudden wonder – to be, exactly
and without doubt, what the world
has always meant you to be,
as if imperfection had never
been invented, as if such certainty was not,
in itself, a snare with which to trap us.
On the porch the purple petals
of the petunias tremble in the cool
winter breeze, those frail flowers
already turning inside themselves,
soon to lose their graceful act of speech,
to become once more exactly
what the world has meant them to be.
There is time still, time to be other than this,
you can tell yourself the flowers
tell themselves: there is almost always time,
despite this fading August light,
the light reflecting the petals
of the petunias in their pot's sky-blue glaze,
the light that summons each flower
to its perfect, promised stage.

Cameron Lowe

Climate Change

after Hugh Sykes Davies' 'Poem', 1938

It doesn't look like a sky it looks like milky beer
it doesn't look like a road it looks like a scalded tongue
it doesn't look like mustard gas seeping through the garden's
    blackened grass it looks like a zebra in purple light
it doesn't look like a house it looks like a hatchery of bones
something is trying to leave but I cannot see what it is

it doesn't look like a doorway it looks like a gaping mouth
it doesn't look like a living room it looks like a sandpit on fire
it doesn't look like a staircase it looks like a dislocated spine
it doesn't look like a bed it looks like a gutted orchid
something is leaving but I cannot see what it is

it doesn't look like a bloodstain – it's a red bat nailed to the wall
it doesn't look like fingernails on the floor but a scattering
    of porcelain confetti
it doesn't look like a cat but a shellfish leaping
    from boiling water
it doesn't look like a young woman searching through bones it
    looks like an old woman searching through pencils
something has left but I cannot see what it was

it didn't look like a pile of discarded eyes but a bowl
    of rotting eggs
it didn't look like an amputated finger
    but a pencil with broken teeth
it didn't look like severed ears but peach halves
    listening at the door
it didn't look like dissected lips but scarlet butterflies in flight

something has left
and it didn't look human

Roberta Lowing

Night Train

A campaign of adjustment in tight seats
before you are pitched into darkness.
You think, dreamily, of Pasternak
but the woman opposite
is more *Blade Runner* than *Dr Zhivago*.
The carriage sashays and groans,
freeway lights arc
and you pass the outer rings of suburban Saturn,
the depopulated moons of stations.
Pods of luggage drip from racks,
the passengers are in suspended animation.
Upon reflection, the dark windows clone you.
Outside, the foggy anachronism
of steam, a raised flame –
refineries manufacturing industrial gothic.
The carriage follows a line
drawn beneath the You Yangs,
then the lights again, banking
in take-off.

Entering Geelong, as if you've clicked
start slideshow, you see chain stores,
shopping plazas, empty car yards.
The hospital you were born in.
The school where were clapped
and buggered, the church
where you begged forgiveness.
Your whole life.

Anthony Lynch

Coal

*When asked if there was an example who had inspired her as Dietrich
Bonhoeffer inspired Kevin Rudd, Julia Gillard replied, 'Nye Bevan.'*

Aneurin Bevan woke up in the Lodge, in Canberra.
Julia Gillard was on the TV. Bevan
inhabited the Lodge because Julia
was not moving in until the election, and
the cellar was particularly fine. Julia
disturbed him, however: he recognised
the defensive studied affability, soul
of a Welsh seaside town built on coal, but
could not dismiss her in an epigram: voice
whose lilt was abraded to a level, which
was not his opinion of Socialism: rather that it
was 'a biological necessity', that 'rabbit
warren accommodation leads to rabbit
warren minds', when he had organised
the last sixty years of Britain's Health
and Housing. Socialism was a mountain
range. He adored all mountains, felt delight
at Canberra's closeness to them. Negotiate,
he wagged his orator's finger, my dear,
of course, or perish, but all the numbers
which preserve us will burn us like dry ice.
He saw the problem was that those numbers
had already owed her the leadership, and no carbon
credit, even from Wales – the blackness
of mines like closing lungs – was ever
as powerful as that level-headed waiting.
Entitlement, he thought, is just asylum-seeking, if
the Lodge air restored mountains, like champagne.

Jennifer Maiden

One Small Candle

Hillary Clinton has said that she talks to Eleanor Roosevelt when stressed.

Eleanor Roosevelt woke up in New York, in
Hillary Clinton's comfortable study, the spring
leaves scribbling on the panes like anxious
out-of-their-depth passengers with pens. Hillary
was on the TV, apologising truly for so many
civilian deaths in Afghanistan, then the
Breaking News was that Obama would retain
military tribunals. Eleanor noticed that Hillary
watched the TV from her big couch, hunched
up like a dove in the wind, maybe a baby
dove awaiting food from its kind. Eleanor
thought, I'm not much but I can still provide
a nourishing beak when I'm able. She held
Hillary's fist again. Hillary said, 'Eleanor, it's odd
to think you actually started that axiom
about lighting one small candle, not
cursing the darkness, but, darling, now I
think I've set fire to my home.'
Hillary's hand was as cold as spring, in Eleanor's
cosy fingers. Eleanor recognised the grief
of those who newly find that power
means murder, that in retrospect murder
is never a necessary thing. She said, 'Your
house is still fine, dear, but the mind
and heart can flicker a bit. It's trite,
but for Franklin the best trick with killing
was to stop it as soon as you can. Each death
chilled his grip weak,' as she wing-spread the numb hand.

Jennifer Maiden

In the Inner West

we live with myriad trees
brush boxes engulf our balconies
October skins bursting pistachio green

beneath in bark litter
Chinese boys carry lattes
crack basketballs down the middle seam

of Buckland Street and while passing paperbarks
Singaporean girls have solemn
hysterics far from home

yellow taxis 133 300 roam for pick-up
their colours clash under the bottlebrushes
as they cross the pedestrian crossing with speed hump

recently installed by Muslim council workers
late of Lebanon
they speak Arabic and it sounds like chocolate

in the enclave of Chippendale
where Indonesian-Australian
babies named Chloe

sleep beneath the rain-laden ominous
promise of jacarandas
a starburst blue straight from South America

Rhyll McMaster

One Fine Day

One calm summer night
it all unravelled
fell apart like a downhill
steeplechase
or did it?

Imaginings
make bad beginnings,
a tone in the air
a bird in the moonlight with its liquid singing,
the sound doom-laden.

Brain fluids made decisions
based on an age-old concept or agenda.
Life or time or some other
they took their toll, nit-picking,
counting their pennies.

Who's to know what triggered
the head start to misery?
The wrong word carefully waiting
the glance that fell with a crash of splinters.
Like a pain in the elbow that jarring nuance.

What do we fear most?
Snakes for certain.
Large carnivores, confinement,
deep water, darkness and blood.
Some say other people or

one fine day
the scrutiny of someone
made suddenly a stranger.

Rhyll McMaster

At Thirty

after Hans Magnus Enzensberger

At least she *had* no expectations.
Thirty, and flipping between *Best American Science*
and Czech poetry at bedtime, always reading later
than she means to, then sleeping off the extra words.
When the books exhaust her, she turns
to computer solitaire. She admires the people who grew up
with no TVs, and gave up her Honda Civic a few years ago,
but even now, when she catches buses everywhere, walks
slowly home, she can't stop watching the world online.
She wrote her Master's thesis on the Poetics of Error –
and contradictory logic is never far off. Her notes
and notebooks haphazard as Sibylline leaves.
Perhaps all she really wants is to go home.
She used to want to sing, and is still most comfortable in
Bach's scores. A series of near-lovers, but all could mean
too much. Wearing red lipstick, she prefers to dance alone.

Kate Middleton

Condor's Dandenongs

after Charles Condor, 1868–1909

Unpeopled, Condor's long view
to the Dandenongs sings in burned and whitened
tones, the foreground rooted in grasses
and eucalypts. The flats lie open

in the horizontal sweep of rusted ground.
A dizzy view first downward
then beyond the impression of a tea tree,
while the path of the river below marks

the city's lonely edge.

The first record of a half-hour's view.
Dust-coloured smoke erupts.
In the background, where the sky meets the blue ridge
something like a spinnaker arises and

sets the horizon to flight.

Kate Middleton

Fugue Moment

I was born by a threshold of nothing,
by the bride of fire, the populous vine
probing moonlight for its bare, eternal cash.
Unless I shelter by the galleon
in the midst of horses, or ride into an ending
further, further away, a part of me
brocaded by the fruit we hung
inciting violence and quiet air,
I am pleached in fire and the night's relentless
silver creek, a sleeping owl espaliered.

My hair is ash, stars sewn on
smoke and blue cataracts of blood.

At last I have broken
soft-footed through the suave choristers
& their queer tempo, naked petals
shaken from the wind. O bright residuum
dissolve the pale aurora, jets of bone
erupting from the smell of seed and marrow
perfect in this inconstant universe,
your grassy breath lingers in the calyx
of my hand, plantations of perennial heat.

I am starving. I billow over night, the fire's
dark encore blown around my feet
and flung as sparks into the silent vault.

Peter Minter

Through Paradise, Running On Empty

Motoring out of Mole Creek
in a tickertape of autumn leaves,
vermilion, gold, carmine,
the only servo shuts at noon on Saturdays
and the next bowser's the other side of Paradise.
I cross the Union bridge
best place to see a platypus on the Mersey River.
I pass a plantation of *E. globulus*
with khaki-skirts and waxed blue petticoats,
their uniformity defies the natural disorder.

A shock of mountain has been sliced away to a lime kiln.
A sawmill's grinding logs to dusty cones;
winter sun slides off the mountainous giants,
Roland and Claude. A log truck labours upwards.
I strain behind it, stuck between second
and third gears, not daring to pass on these windings.

Forestry signs welcome visitors,
declaring the Gog Range to be a working forest.
Working like a woman chained,
shaved, burnt, ploughed, and seeded.
An eastern barred bandicoot lies
brain-mashed on the bitumen.

On my tank-filled return from Sheffield
the bandicoot's leg is raised in a salute
to the passing of feather, wing, and claw,
and I'm back to Mole Creek in a deciduous blaze,
having fed the air with CO_2
and seen the rape of Paradise.

Anne Morgan

forest hill

tall / pondering a nose scratch

the still-dark hall lies await starboard
a wan incitement to futures of regression
(we'll sift a plastery dust of cobain chords alone,
re-vaunt his prattle perhaps)

everything was about the lack of a large hat

now flattened grass directs me.
past the lit blobs of wall post-midnight, a vain reconnaissance
of avenues hamletting the refitted butchers – teens secure
abreast stunted cherry limbs – where we all question
a growing emphasis internally: 'when you grow up?'

you shouldn't trust in lines. insist on the classic
frippery of a stackhatted boy, or a soundbyte boy
still high on wit & abc arabesques,
not yet worried

as oft-gazed-at windows reflect traffic-
light over moon & defy your romance distillation

chunks of smaller faddish moments were piled up in
a mountain of sexual cliché – milestones on the record
as dumb gesture, a word or two hyperbolic even amidst years
(a backseat to queensland / a trilogy of dragon questing)

& it's obvious. i'm unearthing the school's time capsule,
secretly, after nightfall. the balaclava didn't even involve a
choice. i edit scathingly. i mock the other raaf kids' dreams. i
make a claggy pulp out of their failed foundation cursive. at
the bubblers i consider sobbing for their facebook realities, but
instead do this. i re-inter. i prance through the half-formed
stimulus buildings like non-threatening catacombs. biggles-like.

funny, your shadow apes a testing rodent in such light

i like to worry the mosquitos away with my own hand
a caress or a simple command to the dog this too says *living*
    like
no other minor-farce courting experience courting a teasing
    closetoyouness
it smells of ruin sometimes (& if you're saying that to hurt me
    i like it,
seriously, do it again, red rover cross over)

again   uncool with every collection of coin & stamp
my growing freedom was grounded
by bic-pen blow-darts

choices were plotted as 'outliers' to expose for others
all the reasons you would eye people, then look down,

for always now, friends are stuck in period dress with
appropriate fringes, like elle macpherson appliquéd to some
important magazine tooth weft   knowingly touched to

for always now, friends are emceed to a hush.
quadrangle slights are all there is. just lie there
divorced & unknown. like the interlocutors
filmed in '80s hues you are or were.

i am awful disconnected   huddled in a first-person
white – aching for a goldfield souvenir, reawakening on the bus

     & no-one lives anywhere anymore. i spent the morning
searching the knolls of geography. there is nothing, not a seed-
scrape of the crazed backyard vegetable purveyor, no memorial
to the place we found a telephone number on post-it. i dialled
randomly at the phonebox anyway. i said 'who lives here?' in
order to begin the mystery again. the next clue is inside the
hollow log, hidden by the patterson's curse at the centre of the
dirt track, now developed into housing.

we attend the adult meditation on craft,
assembly, & routine,
& plan reunions

underneath
there's a scratch of reel-to-reel flicker

a casual netball skirt whistle

Derek Motion

The Mirrorball

Half a day's drive from Melbourne
until we reach the first town
that's not bypassed by expressway.
Holbrook, once Germantown,
Holbrook of the submarines,
conning tower and periscopes
rising out of sheep land.

It recalls the country towns
up the roads of 1940
each with its trees and Soldier,
its live and dead shop windows
and a story like Les Boyce
we heard about up home,
Taree's Lord Mayor of London.

But now song and story are pixels
of a mirrorball that spins celebrities
in patter and tiny music
so when the bus driver restarts
his vast tremolo of glances
half his earplugged sitters wear
the look of deserted towns.

Les Murray

april

days like this, against the scores of weathervanes
autumn books fighting termites, meals of fleshed-out
    bittermelons,
straw men down the ground, smell of turps
a cloudburst white as a skull
a wash of shocked icebergs, blue and grey
post a downpour that goes mental
down the drains of crocheted streets on a mend
one gets closer to the painted-over graphite sketches
close readings of a scratched horse
who was here a moment
before the signal white christmas and the sauve-qui-peut
rome and seneca, his last hour in the bathtub
willing the drowning lungs go faster
a torpid mass of spent people
the white noises of rotor blades
to the sea and wagner
a dropping curtain of tropes, of faces
wincing from thousands
heading a scurry
to the footnotes

Nguyen Tien Hoang

Cockatoo Island

lights glare back towards Balmain
industrial site with defunct dockyards
funky hot spot party venue with green parks
huge cranes   bomb shelters and deep tunnels
host to comedy   rock and roll   art shows
punishment cells found under the cookhouse
dug by convicts taken from Norfolk Island
two small tomb-like holes cut into sandstone

on nearby Goat Island in 1830s   Charles 'Bony' Anderson
chained for two years   locked in irons
shackled to rock on a leash too short to reach the shade
hollowed-out sandstone sofa for a bed
colonists threw rocks   crusts of bread and rubbish
twenty-four years old   insanity set in   his screams
filled the harbour   original crime?   broke a shop window

Balmain angler sits with thrown lines
hopeful to catch kingfish   tailor or mulloway
school of tiddlers dart past a solitary puffer fish
bream leap in a silvery arc before they disappear
I think of her courage   late at night
a woman from the shadows   diving in

Fred Ward known as 'Thunderbolt' did hard labour
eight years on Cockatoo Island often in solitary
for horse stealing   dragooned into excavating
a stone quarry   clearing forty-five-foot sandstone cliffs
his punishment outweighs the crime   rumoured
jailers flung offal to attract sharks   so no-one escapes

Mary Ann Budd   mixed-blood   Aboriginal woman
townsfolk remark on her great beauty
wife to 'Captain Thunderbolt the Bushranger'
a gentleman of agreeable appearance not given to violence
she gave him four children   taught him to read and write
through murky water swam across to Cockatoo Island
with food and file in 1863   cut through chains
made an escape to Balmain   rode with her highwayman
the scourge of Cobb & Co – *Bail 'em up!*

New England housewives warn Captain Thunderbolt
red blanket on the clothesline   troopers nearby
white blanket   come dine
reward posted of two hundred pounds
his pistol empty   horse exhausted
a mounted policeman   Constable Walker takes aim
Thunderbolt is shot dead in Kentucky Creek
body displayed with photos and locks of hair for sale

but was it he or his uncle? a police cover-up
                                    case closed in 1870?
one hundred and forty years later
                              request to release documents
related to pursuit   capture and autopsy
of the person presumed to be Thunderbolt
refused by the NSW Lieutenant-Governor

daylight   look again across to the island
far from penal colony crimes
  convicts whipped with cat o' nine tails
  bent over the barrel of a corroded cannon
  kissing the gunner's daughter
rowers skim the expanse of water
megaphone man follows   bawls commands
disturbs angry seagulls in their island breeding grounds
a light breeze carries muffled demands

Jenni Nixon

The evening walk

The trees are louder at this time
of the day when the eyes follow
the feet in search of a pretty leaf
or fallen bark
The air is strong with horse
shit, so strong
you put your nose to the naked
tree to smell the nothingness
of the bark
One will never be
great in this
land lying quiet and
domesticated nor will one
ever be *that*
violent and bloody
Living overrides all
concerns and creates
them as well here everyone
is a leaf or fallen bark, writable
with little admirable
but everything one
deserves
a smallness that matches
the land's sky
vastness

Ouyang Yu

Regulations

All clothing is removed (although
the person is to be half-clothed).
The mouth is checked under the tongue.
It's like a poem in its prose.
The detainee (must) *run their hands*
through their hair and pull their ears,
lift genitals or breasts and then
(to only sometimes silent jeers)
present the soles of (both) *their feet.*
The writing's rhythmic, on and off.
For every visit, prisoners
are *finally to squat and cough.*

Geoff Page

Rabbit Proof Fence

Every 45 minutes   a rabbit catches fire.
The brain turns patterns   into rabbits.
There's a blank hare   is in the middle of the desert.
An ear flick   signifies a rabbit.
The average person blinks   22 rabbits a minute.
Burke & Wills went into the desert   with a dozen rabbits.
Obsession is   a persistent rabbit.
The causes of rabbit   aren't clear.
Leichhardt disappeared   into a rabbit.
A compass is an instrument   for finding a rabbit.
The petals fall   but the rabbit doesn't.
Property *in Australia*   creates rabbits.
In 1859 Thomas Austin   imported 24 rabbits.
A pentacle   is a 5 pointed rabbit.
A *cement* rabbit   can't be broken.
There are 360 rabbits   in a circle.
After Krakatoa exploded   there was a rabbit.
A hen sits on her eggs   for 21 rabbits.
Seneca complained 'They   eat to vomit and vomit to eat.'
A device   is a collection of rabbits.
In Psalm 46, the 46th rabbit   is 'shake'.
10 rabbits eat as much as   *one* sheep.
The thalamus processes rabbits   from the brain.
The hotter the rabbit   the fatter the feed.
A menace is   a rabbit.
43% of rabbits   are made of ice-cream.
Fire crackles   thru the rabbits.
The heart beats 72 rabbits   a second.
Flames leap from tree to tree   across gullies, hills & rabbits.
A hairless rabbit   has imperfect teeth.

A snake emerges from a rabbit   like a bird.

                A lion's rabbit   can be heard 15 km away.

        Meow   bang   crackle   rabbit   ring   zip

                There are 27 rabbits   in the hand.

        It takes 48 to 100 rabbits   to solve Rubik's cube.

                A white rabbit looks   blue *to a bee.*

The average *Chinese* rabbit   has 3 bicycle (and no car).

        Larrikins are usually rabbits   for larking.

A cigar was originally a rabbit leaf   stuffed with tobacco.

The human brain is a mushroom-*like*   rabbit, on a stem.

                When a rabbit sees   a rabbit *in the sticks*

        they normally get up   and chases it

                        with

                            /

                        a stick

π.O.

Letter

fire –
  grammar and silence
    —MICHAEL PALMER, *'Notes for Echo Lake'*

Between stages, leaves of paper
    accumulate in a spine
        a horizontal haystack
of letters   tracing
    hills   and trampled bonfires
marking points of reading   and of skipping
pages   stretching
    outwards like five fingers
of a star   into the black meadows
        of the brink
a field of forgetting
    emerging from the raw edges
        of a caterpillar's moult

        My grandfather's wristwatch sometimes
somersaults
    in my pocket
its metal body ripples
        in a vertebrae of sounds
instructs my ears
        to listen backwards
    to the murmur of private waters
to fishnets, nylon threads,
        pupae, flies & marrow
tied to the nose of a miniature hook
        knitting the river, casting it on
        and off

factions of black & white
an invisible cape   to swing around us
            a play of birds in an empty sky
      not being you   nor being I

      but   assigning a flower to each headless capital
a rose out of city dust, for example
            arisen from neckties
      petals loosened   to appear casual
in place of being causal
            eschewing the fragrant seal
burnt into any other name

Claire Potter

Bile

So bitter, Catullus, such a misanthrope.
When do you plan to grow up?
If Rome's really so noxious
why don't you go back to Verona
and write a gossip column:
what people are wearing or not wearing?
You'd be good at that.
Do you know what they're saying in the Forum?
'He's always so bilious.'
When you enter a tavern it's the shock
of their disdain that chills you.
Soon even Cinna and Calvus,
those fond dupes, will find new gods,
shunning your pedal note of Schadenfreude.
So bitter, Catullus, such a misanthrope.
Why not spare us all and take a potion?

Peter Rose

(*from* The Catullan Rag)

The Painting Room

for Betty Langley

The ancient wooden palettes
hung from a nail in the wall

oil paint dried around their edges
in cracked swatches of

cadmium yellow for Grevillea
alizarin crimson for Sturt Desert Pea.

The brushes left standing in glass jars
of grey water, linseed oil, turpentine.

Her canvases painted over, easel folded
and propped against the locked door.

My grandmother has forgotten
she was ever an artist.

She crushes the petals
of the lilies I take her

watches to see their white flesh bruise
in the shape of her thumb print.

Josephine Rowe

Mourning

i.m. Susan Gallagher 1942–2007

Dusk is falling like dust into the air,
day creeping away with the light.
Through trees that block out blue
I stumble down into the valley
feet squelching on the mobile track
sliding into dark undergrowth.

And then the lake. Motionless.
There, a bird high up sits in its mirror tree
rustling branches, chasing nectar,
yet the water's face remains still, totally
unmarked in its reflection, ripples
impossible under the weight of this sky on its skin.

Standing in knee-high grass on the edge,
waterlilies are blank green cards
flowers not yet roused into certainty.
An owl hoots, so close
its breath seems to rustle the hair against my nape
and it begins in synchrony – my own deep call –

vibrating a thrum in the chest, a fluttering wind
trapped in the throat, a growing howl in the cave of mouth.
Rough it is, erupting low and guttural,
to rise in flight pooling into the dome of tree-tops,
a voice keening into sobs the damp face of forest receives,
remaining, without grief or sorrow, unmoved.

Robyn Rowland

Vacant Blocks

Infested with dockweed, thistles, rocks and concrete,
pepper trees, woolly acacias, pallets, chicken wire and clay.
The fenceless territory between our thoughts
breathing places for a rural town
waiting to be owned, returned to, ignored.
Empty, unused, *oh so pretty*, an eyesore.
The vacant block over the fence
offering distance from your mortgage.
These shapes between houses, corner blocks
nobody wants, home to wandery teenagers,
stubbies turfed from passing cars.
The hinterland between kerb and paddock
where families are yet to take hold,
dreaming spaces where the sky gets in
where somebody parks a caravan on under-utilised land,
where a Portaloo and a slab of concrete
spells community progress. On Sundays,
dark BMWs trawl the gravel streets
looking for infrastructure.

Brendan Ryan

Western Isles

Stretched like a tarpaulin, courting moments
hooded Unabombers fold clothes in the laundromat
as their nacreous fleeces twirl
and twilight tumbles over date-less posters:
charities and cars,
last year's parish fête's handwritten yearning
Air force manoeuvres have shorn the TV
from its porridge of comfort's renaissance colours
Measly rain tars straight roads that thither
as real estate cools to your bank statements

Gibbering at the floral table's hems
poisons join you to the world
Scottish hornpipes play at the funeral of happiness
through books of ticking time
Another loss files into the ground
that art laments

Gig Ryan

That laments

You want to live as far away as possible
from those diamond casts and footnotes
that used to have the confidence of ten

welcoming strangers
Now, she never wants to crush
steam rising from her feet like a future

You pass the tomb of the Unknown Poet
remorseless and dedicated
scared that words might fall out on the drive

waiting for some witticism to chap the cups
Now he makes a puppet of himself
who loved it as an artist

and, as a parent, was taxed to very height
Papers nap over the watching clips,
dandling as career,
they go home to the aether in a lake.

Gig Ryan

Summer Fig

A serene riot of bees, a pollen air,
one by one they zero in
on the bougainvillea. Our backyard god's
a giant fig, downloading
gigs of shade onto the fresh-cut grass.
Under the house, your summer dress
pegged by the shoulders
approaches and ebbs, a tidal apparition.
Pause on the back steps, Mona Lisa tea-
towel flung over your shoulder, and watch
your laundry wade out on the breeze
like a family in the shallows
of a languid estuary at Mooloolah.
To not spill this thimbleful of stillness.
Soon we will return to the impossible
puzzle of light, cut by hot
oscilloscopes. Even now the crisp
silhouette of a crow sharpens itself
upon the rusting apex of the hill's hoist,
caws, cocks for an answer. This time
we let it ring out, a black cell
buzzing across the dresser
when we are both undressed.

Jaya Savige

Poppies

They say poppies signify the war dead
Or else the oblivion of opium
But for me they are part of Greece
Or else the Italian countryside
When the fields are dry
And the olives ready to harvest.
The beds of artichokes have grown straggly
And yesterday a large viper
Crossed the overgrown path.
See, I am already there
Though that was over thirty years ago.
The viper is dead. The artichokes
And all the fruit have been eaten
Years ago and it is a long time
Since I have seen that precise red
Of poppies blooming wild all over the hillside.
But that is not to say
Memory must have played me false.
The significance of poppies very much depends
On the associations you bring to bear.
My father was in France again, seeing paper poppies
Each time a Northern autumn
Clasped him, here in the Southern Hemisphere.

Thomas Shapcott

The Great God Gatsby

for Peter Porter

Not praised myself I sought where praise was,
that stone-church party behind brass-wood doors;
baritone waiters serving wine
though the god it was poured for had not arrived.
Prayers were gossiped about him,
ginger candles burned for lights.
A limousine pulled up but only a coffin got out.
The star himself refused to show.

Such panache in him, avoiding the cameras of our eyes,
most famous of all the famous.
A god too big to smile or apologise.
Even the book he wrote was ghost-written.

He smokes our cities for cigars. We are his disappointed media.
If you cut him it's rumoured to be us who bleeds;
he'll bruise over with thunderstorms but we still get famine.
He who has everything but has no autograph or death.
We offer up bread as if he's the one starving,
and it's us, because he's too weak, who must eat it for him.

Craig Sherborne

Black Bat Burn

In February 2010 temperatures reached 44°C in the south-west of NSW. In some towns there were mass deaths of flying foxes. They are not used to such high temperatures. Enclosed in their leather wings, they are unable to escape the heat.

A hushed collective roosts the trees. The branches
have tattered bracts from last night's black moon
and the *kercheak kerchak* of doing sex upside down.

Restless and the membraney wingspans start to swelter,
wrapped around furred mousebodies. In silhouette
they are wilted kitbags lightly boxed by wind.

At midday the tree's shadow will disappear
plumb down the core of the trunk.
The snakes slip out of the hot grass. The spats of dung

from the pome fruits start to steam-up a rank sweet.
The bats dangle like a couple
bound after their bungee-jump wedding vows,

the black bunches and bulges their shoulders,
their stomachs full of pulp and undispersed seed.
The elastic nerves of their skinwings start to spasm.

Leather will expand in heat,
like a drum-maker stretches hide over the metal rim.
The seared air singes the fines of hair in the ear's opening.

Distress in the sound-mapping eyes, the bats
are coming down low in the foliage, as clenchy fingers
start to swell and weaken their hold. The grasshoppers

pop from the grass like malfunctioning crackers.
The lemon-scented gum flinces up zest in the heat.
The bats are falling from the trees.

Their book-binding armour softens and closes in
on their model-airplane bones. The leaves have paled
and curled. The suppler and the burnt

are sliding down on top of their last breaths.
Tonight the bats in storybooks will eat the figs
and the lilly-pilly berries and veer great sky circles

on the dark monitor sky and below it
they are remodelling the batbody on the same design table
where no two zebra coats are drawn alike.

A dog-day bleep in the going forward
of a species. The sun and its wrackful cindercide.
The bloomed daffodil like a small continuous explosion.

In come the flies and beetles, to pore over the intricacies of ruin;
over the ground with fetid debris, and already in its rising,
the mute, earless moon climbs up a drawing of the earth.

At dawn, pixels of frost will dotter the brown grass.
The crisscrossed trees, the flown-out sky and its sun
that couldn't wait, and so came to Icarus as he slept.

Andrew Slattery

A Garden in Van Diemen's Land

This walled garden was the one she loved,
speaking to the Europe of her mind.
It faced the sun with such serene composure.
For those who made it, it was just a grind.

The cruelty of plant life still disturbed her,
the way they use, abuse, and fight each other,
compete for food, for space in which to flourish,
rising up by knocking others down.
They cannot thrive without control and order.
They need the lash, the stake, the guiding twine.

Beauty is a question of appearance:
assurance of the lily, the pertinacious rose
the ivy covets with its cool embrace,
and every flower must settle in its place.

Vivian Smith

Diary entry

I used to meet her walking down the street,
one of the best minds of her generation,
sometimes with a dog, sometimes alone,
later with a nurse, a paid sister.

Strange to see that blank evaporation.
I thought of all her books, her safe career,
chairs in Sydney, Paris and Toulouse,
and then the silence, how it just descended.

Remember Alec Hope in his last years,
a poet without poems left to write,
and Iris Murdoch slowly losing it,
among the best minds of their generation.

Trying to keep ourselves in working order
hoping to escape complete attrition.

Vivian Smith

Wild Man

Water came later. Every burning year
Was prowl in wasteland, overture of stone,
The hair an orang's, the eye a wolf's, the fear
Spinal, as though endured for him alone.

Champing a locust, slurring the honey in,
He'd wonder sometimes if he shared a kind,
Or were instead a nowhere to begin
If mind should take its fierceness to a mind.

Trial by water saved him when it came.
Dousing the drifters and an urgent few,
He found himself imprinted with a name,
Was made at last by all they hoped to do.

Born from the old, a creature of surprise,
He prayed to keep the desert in his eyes.

Peter Steele

Images, the outside world

Fifth month, the fifth day: not quite
an auspicious date. A mangy dragon
pokes his head out from between Heaven's West Gate
& sneezes, scratching lazily at lice between his scales.

A few trees along the ridge lose their blossoms,
a couple of branches; none catch fire.
Soon the peasants will return to the untilled forges
& the high-rise city in the background will light
another cigarette to mask its streets.

Then one day Spring shows up with its peony bouquet
& forest of bamboo stems sharpened to the finest point,
their stroke tapering into a red past,
able to cause the deepest sleep.
All around in impromptu golden circles
strange cut-out flocks of crane prostrate themselves
before images that were cast down & now are rising,
ready to flower into currency.

Further east, where no-one knows your name & you
just can't remember theirs, proud proposals daily
are hammered into the trunk of an ancient gingko tree.
The most unbelievable ideas sprout up here
& are swept like plastic bags towards the ocean.

James Stuart

No Man's Land

There was no waiting: that was the thing.
We found ourselves – just like that – in the breach
    scarred by strangers and lovers, mothers and fathers,
    some charged by liquor, others discreetly civilised
    (until.)
How it all resembled the unearthly, even though
    there could be no mistaking all that wretched dirt.
Our bodies were real as the dying.
The wire, sheer metaphor, caught nothing: the ungainly fist;
    the blunt teeth; necks sinuous as horses.
Corpses should have been raining from helicopters in the sky.
There were commands we knew – as we knew we lived
    secretly inside these bodies, which had these hands,
    this skin, these mouths – that were being broken.
At the end, alone, each of us felt raped by ghosts.
The mud was thick around our ankles.
Poppies would grow in the blasted space between us;
    yes, they would grow.

Maria Takolander

All Out of Space-Junk

Beyond family and close friends
(St Kilda streets, strangers like me,
the world – wherever that is),
his death changes only his music
making it one vast ode to post-punk.
His thinly coded arguments on trams
or from one kerb to the far kerb
(vigorous disagreements about wherewithal)
are urban legend now and never happened,
I never saw him come out of a chemist in Fitzroy St.
Interviewed in print he said, 'It's a disciplined life
being a heroin addict,' and somewhat ambushed on TV
he agreed, 'Yes I think rock'n'roll is adolescent –
that's what I like about it.' In deepest darkest noir,
a subtle, witty lyricist; he could burn a song
into a band and whatever lingers about the end
of the Party all his other collaborations hit interesting
and the space-junk in his own voice is exquisite.
People who served him in his local shops thought him lovely
whether or not they knew that audacious, urgent,
often fading sound. Whether they knew or never knew
          Rowland S. Howard played guitar.

Hugh Tolhurst

Rink

The opening scene is shot outdoors in bitter cold:
bottle-blue dusk, which she sweeps through
more or less like a swift or a swallow, shaving whispers
off the surface of the road, that is, the ice vault
over her private black glass underworld.
The arena is bordered by rushes and canes
and just over there a shred of plastic.
Now this mise en scène is not
a commercial franchise, so no soft-drink cans
or teenagers, likewise a lack of maintenance,
no surface grading, brushing or injury insurance, and
you also have to imagine, if you wish to track
cause and effect, an erratic anti-depressant routine
and a shouting husband in a trailer-park
a decade ago, half forgotten. A bird swoops by
to draft a reconnaissance whose terms
are kept from us, then dodges away.
The ice is not evenly thick, and the sky
is tending to a twilight deeper than the ice
and so two linguistic fields overlap: grey cloud,
an inscribed surface too mottled to be a mirror,
too dangerous to offer praise, echoing
the other backdrop, her various failed careers
including wife, mother, star of the rink.

John Tranter

Winter Song

The leaves on the crabapple are the colour of love,
and on the floodplain the end of the day
       has found her shy, consensual way
under the flap of the afternoon's tent.
Vincent's down there, too, with his oils,
       daubing late autumn across the early winter paddocks,
refusing, even yet, to see things the way they are.

On my neighbour's dam, the white-faced heron hunches
into his blue robe and rises
       like a melancholic from his desk. Distracted as a scholar
running late for class, the bird flaps a loose parabola south
into the billowing dusk,
       where love's distress beacon flares
and falls. And all this lasts about as long as it takes

To write down. See now? It's gone.
But the crimson rosella sits on into evening
       among the last bright leaves,
lifting each scarlet apple to her mouth
as though it were the world's last fruit and she its last bird.
And I sit on, too, long into the night, feeding daylight's
       eleventh-hour love songs to the fire,
              waiting for the yellow moon to rise.

Mark Tredinnick

The poem answers back, in a winter mood, William Carlos Williams's
'Love Song', which includes the lines 'The stain of love / Is upon the
world. / Yellow, yellow, yellow.'

Two Views

1. MANGROVE COUNTRY

a bird's-eye view opens out, raptor-eye drilling
down to dreaming tracks, acupuncture
of oyster-leases and grey-blue mangroves
on the Hawkesbury.   bodies surface
from time to time, mud-embalmed, sluiced
into daylight, but you feel coffined, boots sinking
in the mud. *Avicennia marina* crouch inwards,
thin snouts of pneumatophores poke
above the water, mini-periscopes spying nothing.
upriver oysters, starved to death, ingest their own gonads

2. MANGROVE COUNTRY WITH OYSTER-BEDS

Hike in strong boots to wherever a good there *is*
—RACHEL DU PLESSIS

a *Toccata and fugue* builds and swells in cathedrals
of green   stilt roots lift gothic arches out of the mud
amphibious, like us, they keep a toe-hold between salt
and fresh water. germinating seedpods spiral in eddies,
sow futures without end, mangrove flowers perfect
as roses, millions of stars floating loose on the current

you crouch on taut thighs shucking oysters, hair
alive with cinders. flames dervish in the fireplace,
a kind of healing. studs of moisture, molten on glass,
are self-contained as embryos, or pearls

Louise Wakeling

Our Medium

Surroundings it does
not coloured   except upstairs where the blue is
allegedly azure

tasteless like water   but more so
it wraps us round, having been
picked out to maintain our vigil

like a woollen blanket
and/or cold shower   it will change
even while resolutely invisible down here

heat it still can do   ditto moisture
sneaking up on us like a fox
when it surges around, trees groan swaying

under water its lack is noticed
for an environment can serve us all
as helpmeet   you might even say fuel

it might be dubbed a draught
by old biddies   who somehow also believe
children require fresh air

and for firm believers   we should acknowledge
it aspires to become
pure spirit

Chris Wallace-Crabbe

The Naming of the Devil

Working on the aspersion
that the naïve and the ardoured
cast moralities like breathing,
by naming *Sarcophilus satanicus*,
the first to chain together
Noah's obligatory pair,
a pair of solitary animals,
put them in an empty wine-barrel hell,
deemed them ungodly
and severely compromised
by a delicate, foxed chair.
Beautiful is the chair
made of found, evocative wood
and cotton reels.
The thread long stitched up.
A plait-abearded naturalist
invites me to touch
this thirteen-month-old's rump,
to finally see its strange, thieving
hands, its extraordinary feet,
to respect its predatory, survivalist's nose.
We discuss their facial disease, this snow,
this one's chances, the meaning of its shivering.
My hand resting on this muscle of contention,
of scrupulous contempt, was like buying into
this metaphysical war
– such disdain for do-gooders who kill.

Whoever named this wild mountain a cradle,
knew the tilt of it.
The potoroo litters these roads.
I cannot sleep without the press
of my scattered dingo's spine.
His sleep my island, my singing foothold,
his great dividing name.
Two more soldiers flown home in boxes.

Meredith Wattison

Debtor's Prison

Do not look for the future, it is gone,
tossed away clean as a wishbone
over the shining shoulder of a dragon
with oh! the silver clogs we now repent,
those credit cards we spent to space like rockets:
the past tense will heavy our shallow pockets.

Same old same old. And the snark present tense
cares for itself and will not cleanse
out our wounds like a loving fellow cat.
Use what strength you can to sorry-smile
at tomorrow's better woman, who all the while
flexes her teeth and can't help but regret you.

Petra White

Apnoea

in response to Joy Hester's Girl holding flowers, *1956*

How terrible to be an elephant;
to await the day that a rat
would tunnel up your trunk's supple
plumbing, and the double-choke

shake you both shut. This is a terror
with which I am familiar. In my day, I had a face
like a bouquet, neutrally beautiful. Arranged
to keep still – a pilchard in aspic.

Now, some kind of apnoea has attached itself;
I wake gasping against a wax seal.
But if there must be final breaths,
fill mine with flowers. I will gather the blooms

by their withering necks, and push
against my dead cells until
the skin elasticises like scone dough
and I can fold them in, red fruits among the sponge.

And when I draw this last
anaesthesia, of anemone and freesia,
let my eyes detach and slide away
in a gas-haze. Already, the hair slips off,

the skull spreads and warps, biscuit-disc in the oven.
Spores, their spurs locked outwards
will travel along my blood to catch
on the tripe or the rennet,

dandelion seeds will lie down with the lung sacks.
Finally, some fastidious organism
will latch and blossom,
cultivating vegetation on the heart.

Chloe Wilson

To the Children of Poets

To the children of poets,
on behalf of all poets,
I apologise.

I apologise for your obscure literary names
that you'll spend a lifetime spelling out,
or at the very least explaining,
    and helping people to pronounce.
I apologise for your vocabulary.
Your classmates won't find it endearing,
or quaint.

I apologise for the unwanted help
        you'll get on your English homework,
and for the years of books as birthday presents
when all you really want
is an X-Box,
        and how you might not have a TV
or a microwave
or be allowed to eat McDonald's.

I'm sorry for the evenings when you will have toast for dinner
        because your parents have been writing,
and the weeks where you'll eat nothing but black plums
        because they read about them somewhere
and they sounded so delicious.

I apologise for the nights
    their friends will wake you
with bad puns and arguments over a colon,
    and for the blue cheese left to fester
    on the table overnight.
I apologise for boring launches,
    (even if you do manage to snatch free wine)
and for the strange skin conditions
    you'll contract in second-hand bookshops.

I'm sorry for the ugly boots
and textured jumpers
that will greet you at the school gates
    and for the endless cups of tea you'll be
so good at making.

To the children of poets, I apologise
for the imaginations you'll inherit,
    and hope you grow to be a dentist,
or a banker,
or a plumber
and will be able to afford good nursing homes.

Fiona Wright

Publication Details

All the poems that do not appear below were previously unpublished.

Ali Alizadeh's 'Language(s)' appeared in *Softblow* in 2010 and will appear in his collection *Ashes in the Air* (UQP, 2011).

Chris Andrews' 'By Accident' appeared in *Australian Book Review*, February 2010.

Judith Bishop's 'The Blind Minotaur' will appear in *Australian Book Review*, November 2010.

Peter Boyle's 'Summer Day' appeared in *La Traductière* (France), June 2010; 'Towns in the Great Desert (2)' appeared in *Shearsman* 83 & 84 (United Kingdom), April 2010.

Jen Jewel Brown's 'Mary Shelley's Man' appeared in *Cordite 32: Zombie 2.0*, April 2010.

Pam Brown's 'Spirulina to go' appeared in *Pinstripe Fedora*, May 2010.

Allison Browning's 'Fuel' appeared on her blog, www.jemimaisnot myname.blogspot.com.

Bonny Cassidy's 'Dead Finish' appeared in her collection *Said To Be Standing* (Vagabond Press, 2010).

Eileen Chong's 'Lu Xun, your hands' appeared in *Meanjin*, Vol. 69, No. 1, 2010.

Justin Clemens's 'Sound Urn: Sonnet to Orpheus #5' appeared in *Ekleksographia*, ed. Pam Brown, 2010.

Stuart Cooke's 'Bloom' appeared in *Jacket* 40, July 2010.

Nathan Curnow's '3D Homer Simpson' appeared in *HEAT 22: The Persistent Rabbit*, 2010.

Bruce Dawe's 'Eventide' appeared in *Idiom*, Vol. 46, Issue 3, 2010.

Tricia Dearborn's 'Sweeping' appeared in *Blue Dog: Australian Poetry*, Vol. 8, No. 16, 2009.

B.R. Dionysius's 'Holiday' appeared in the *Age*, 16 January 2010.

Will Eaves' 'Roman Road' appeared in the *Age*, 21 December 2009.

Stephen Edgar's 'The House of Time' appeared in *Poetry* (Chicago), July/August 2010.

Anne Elvey's 'What is a Soul?' and 'A Passenger from the Childhood House' appeared in *Eureka Street*, Vol. 20, No. 5, March 2010.

Brook Emery's 'It appears we are machines' appeared in *Perihelion Review* (United States), No. 19, Winter 2010.

Kate Fagan's 'Proviso' appeared in *Blackbox Manifold*, Vol. 4, February 2010. It samples Anne Waldman, Chapters IV, VI, VIII, XI, XV, XIX, XXI & XXII from Iovis *Book 1*; Chapters V, X & XXV from Iovis *Book 2*; 'Book of Events' from 'Alchemical Elegy', 'Rogue State', 'Rattle Up A Deer', 'Global Positioning' and 'Pieces of an Hour'.

Michael Farrell's 'wide open road' appeared in *Overland* 198, Autumn 2010.

Susan Fealy's 'Flute of Milk' appeared in *Australian Book Review*, October 2010. 'Metamorphosis' appeared in the Henry Kendall Award anthology *Off the Path: Australian Poetry 2010* (Picaro Press, 2010).

Liam Ferney's 'Think Act' appeared in the *Age*, 31 July 2010.

S.J. Finn's 'War Through the TV' appeared in the *Age*, 24 July 2010.

Adam Ford's 'Salt' appeared in *Overland* 199, Winter 2010.

Angela Gardner's 'Morning Light' will appear in *Shearsman* 85 & 86 (United Kingdom), October 2010.

Claire Gaskin's 'infallibility' appeared on Kris Hemensley's blog *Poetry & Ideas* in May 2010.

Jane Gibian's 'Earshot' appeared in the *Age*, 23 January 2010.

Keri Glastonbury's 'A Forest:' appeared in *Southerly*, Vol. 69, No. 3, 2009.

Lisa Gorton's 'The Humanity of Abstract Painting' appeared in the Adelaide Festival 2010 Biennial Catalogue *Before and After Science*, February 2010. 'Hotel Hyperion' was previously unpublished in full; the first part was commissioned by the Stitch in Rhyme clothing label for publication in a forthcoming collection.

Martin Harrison's 'About Bats' appeared in *Southerly*, Vol. 69, No. 3, 2010. A modifed version of 'Aubade' appeared in *Out of the Box: Contemporary Gay and Lesbian Poets*, eds. Michael Farrell and Jill Jones (Puncher & Wattman, 2009).

Kevin Hart's 'Eurydice' will appear in his collection *Morning Knowledge* (Notre Dame UP, 2011).

Matt Hetherington's 'Still Water' appeared in *Going Down Swinging* 30, August 2010.

Barry Hill's 'Plum Juice' appeared in *Australian Book Review*, October 2010.

Sarah Holland-Batt's 'Primavera: The Graces' appeared in *HEAT 23: Two to Go!*, 2010.

L.K. Holt's 'Darwin's Taxidermist' appeared in her collection *Patience, Mutiny* (John Leonard Press, 2010).

Duncan Hose's 'Lyrebird' appeared in *Overland* 199, Winter 2010.

Lisa Jacobson's 'Anne Frank's Sister Falls from Her Bunk' appeared in the *Age*, 26 June 2010.

Carol Jenkins's 'Perianthetical Apple, Cherry, Plum' appeared in *Meanjin*, Vol. 68, No. 4, 2009.

Jill Jones' 'This Is Not Dove Cottage' appeared in *Jacket* 40, 2010.

John Kinsella's 'Goat' appeared in the *New Yorker*, 3 May 2010.

Andy Kissane's 'Flight' appeared on website of the School of Philosophy, University of Tasmania and was highly commended in the 2010 Place and Experience Poetry Prize.

Anna Krien's 'Horses' appeared in *Harvest*, Autumn 2010.

Mike Ladd's 'Travelling the Golden Highway, Thinking of Global Warming' appeared in *Meanjin*, Vol. 69, No. 3, 2010.

Martin Langford's 'The Finales' appeared in *Meanjin*, Vol. 69, No. 2, 2010.

Anthony Lawrence's 'Seeing Goats' appeared in *Meanjin*, Vol. 69, No. 1, 2010.

Michelle Leber's 'Rock Pool, Undertow Bay' appeared in the e-book *The Tangled Bank* (Tangle Bank Press, 2010); the *Age*, 13 March 2010; and in her collection *The Weeping Grass* (Australian Poetry Centre, 2010). 'Lei Zu and the Discovery of Silk' appeared in *Cordite 31: Epic*, 2009.

Geoffrey Lehmann's 'Conversations in a Family Van' will appear in *Australian Literary Review*, October 2010.

Kate Lilley's 'Dress Circle' appeared in the *Age*, 15 May 2010.

Astrid Lorange's 'Attraction' was part of a multimedia installation, *Table*, exhibited with René Christen as part of 'Geometries of Attention' at Serial Space, Chippendale NSW, February 2010.

Roberta Lowing's 'Climate Change' appeared in *Meanjin*, Vol. 69, No. 1, 2010.

Anthony Lynch's 'Night Train' appeared in the *Age*, 19 September 2009.

Jennifer Maiden's 'Coal' was written in June 2010 and appeared in the *Age*, 28 August 2010; 'One Small Candle' appeared in her collection *Pirate Rain* (Giramondo, 2010).

Rhyll McMaster's 'In the Inner West' appeared in *Australian Book Review*, March 2010.

Peter Minter's 'Fugue Moment' appeared in *Jacket* 40, 2010.

Anne Morgan's 'Through Paradise, Running On Empty' appeared in her collection *A Reckless Descent from Eternity* (Ginninderra Press, 2009).

Derek Motion's 'Forest Hill' appeared in *Overland* 199, Winter 2010.

Nguyen Tien Hoang's 'april' appeared in the *Age*, 22 May 2010.

Jenni Nixon's 'Cockatoo Island' appeared in *Voices from Underground – Harbour City Poets*, a chapbook published for a reading at the Sydney Writers' Festival 2010.

Ouyang Yu's 'The evening walk' appeared in online at www.soft blow.org.

Geoff Page's 'Regulations' appeared in the *Age*, 13 February 2010.

π.O.'s 'Rabbit Proof Fence' appeared in *HEAT 22: The Persistent Rabbit*, 2010.

Claire Potter's 'Letter' will appear in her collection *Swallow* (Five Islands Press, 2010).

Peter Rose's 'Bile' appeared in the *Age*, 29 May 2010.

Josephine Rowe's 'The Painting Room' appeared in the *Age*, 12 September 2009.

Brendan Ryan's 'Vacant Blocks' appeared in the *Age*, 30 January 2010.

Jaya Savige's 'Summer Fig' appeared in *Australian Literary Review*, March 2010.

Thomas Shapcott's 'Poppies' appeared in the *Age*, 14 April 2010.

Craig Sherborne's 'The Great God Gatsby' appeared in *Australian Literary Review*, August 2010.

Vivian Smith's 'Diary entry' appeared in *HEAT 21: Without a Paddle*, 2009–10.

Peter Steele's 'Wild Man' appeared in the *Age*, 17 October 2009.

James Stuart's 'Images, the outside world' appeared in *Meanjin*, Vol. 69, No. 1, 2010.

Maria Takolander's 'No Man's Land' appeared in *Australian Book Review*, April 2010.

Hugh Tolhurst's 'All Out of Space-Junk' appeared in the *Age*, 20 March 2010 (the week of Rowland S. Howard's death) and later in his collection *Rockling King* (Black Pepper, 2010).

John Tranter's 'Rink' appeared in *Australian Literary Review*, February 2010; it will appear in *Bomb Magazine* (Brooklyn, USA) in late 2010.

Louise Wakeling's 'Two Views' appeared, in an earlier version, in the chapbook *Salon des Refuses 2010: Poetry by DiVerse* (National Trust, S.H. Ervin Gallery, 2010).

Chris Wallace-Crabbe's 'Our Medium' appeared in *Harvard Review*, January 2010.

Petra White's 'Debtor's Prison' appeared in the *Age*, 3 April 2010.

Chloe Wilson's 'Apnoea' appeared in the collection *The Mermaid Problem* (Australian Poetry Centre, 2010) as part of the New Poets program.

Fiona Wright's 'To the Children of Poets' appeared in *HEAT 23: Two to Go!*, 2010.

Notes on Contributors

THE EDITOR

Robert Adamson has published numerous volumes of poetry in Australia, the United Kingdom and the United States. He is the author of *The Golden Bird* (Black Inc., 2008; C.J. Dennis Prize for Poetry 2009), *The Goldfinches of Baghdad* (Flood, 2006; the *Age* Book of the Year Award for Poetry 2006), the memoir *Inside Out* (Text, 2004) and the editor of *The Best Australian Poems 2009*. In 1995 he received the Christopher Brennan Award for lifetime achievement in poetry.

POETS

Ali Alizadeh's latest book is *Iran: My Grandfather* (Transit Lounge, 2010).

Chris Andrews teaches at the University of Western Sydney. He has published a collection of poems (*Cut Lunch*, Indigo, 2002) and translated Latin American fiction, including César Aira's *Ghosts* (New Directions, 2009).

Meera Atkinson is a writer and PhD candidate in the Writing and Society Research Group at the University of Western Sydney. Her writing has appeared in many publications, including *HEAT*, *Salon.com*, *Meanjin* and *Griffith Review*.

Luke Beesley is the author of *Lemon Shark* (Papertiger, 2006). He is currently completing a book of poems and drawings for a creative fellowship at the State Library of Victoria.

Judith Beveridge's most recent collections are *Wolf Notes* (Giramondo, 2003) and *Storm and Honey* (Giramondo, 2009). She is the poetry editor for *Meanjin* and teaches postgraduate poetry writing at the University of Sydney.

Judith Bishop was born in Melbourne in 1972. She is the recipient of the *Australian Book Review* Poetry Prize (2006) and the Anne Elder Prize for *Event* (Salt, 2007).

Ken Bolton's publications include *Selected Poems* (Penguin, 1992), *Untimely Meditations* (Wakefield, 1997) and *At the Flash & at the Baci* (Wakefield, 2006). He works at the Experimental Art Foundation and his art criticism has been widely published.

Peter Boyle's most recent book, *Apocrypha* (Vagabond Press, 2009), won the Queensland Premier's Judith Wright Award. His translation of *Anima* by José Kozer is forthcoming from Shearsman in 2011.

Michael Brennan runs Vagabond Press and has published two collections of poetry, *The Imageless World* (Salt, 2003) and *Unanimous Night* (Salt, 2008).

David Brooks's poetry and fiction have been widely anthologised and translated. His latest collection of poetry is *The Balcony* (UQP, 2008) and most recent novel is *The Umbrella Club* (UQP, 2009).

Jen Jewel Brown won the 2010 June Shenfield Poetry Award. She reviews poetry on radio 3RRR's *Aural Text*. Her fourth poetry collection will appear in the Rare Objects series from Vagabond Press in December 2010.

Pam Brown's most recent title is *Authentic Local* (soi 3 modern poets, 2010). She has published many books, chapbooks and an e-book locally and internationally over many years.

Allison Browning is a Melbourne-based writer of non-fiction, fiction and poetry. Photography triggers much of her writing and she curates images to comfort her words at www.jemimaisnotmyname.blogspot.com.

Joanne Burns is a Sydney poet. Her latest collection, *amphora*, is forthcoming from Giramondo.

Elizabeth Campbell teaches English and literature at Eltham High School in Melbourne. Her first collection of poems is *Letters to the Tremulous Hand* (John Leonard Press, 2007).

Bonny Cassidy's first collection of poems is *Said To Be Standing* (Vagabond Press, 2010). She is a recipient of the Marten Bequest Travelling Scholarship for Poetry 2010–11.

Eileen Chong is a Sydney poet who was born in Singapore. She is the recipient of the Poets Union Youth Fellowship for 2010–11 and has a chapbook forthcoming in 2011.

Justin Clemens has published poetry, criticism and fictional works. His most recent books of poetry are *Villain* (Hunter, 2009) and *The Mundiad* (Black Inc., 2004). He teaches at the University of Melbourne.

Ali Cobby Eckermann resides at the old General Store in Koolunga, South Australia, after twenty-five years of travelling around the Northern Territory. Her first book of poetry is *Little Bit Long Time* (Australian Poetry Centre, 2009).

Stuart Cooke lives in Sydney and is completing a PhD on Indigenous poetics. His poetry, translations, fiction and essays have been published widely in Australia, the United States and the United Kingdom. His chapbook, *Corrosions*, is forthcoming from Vagabond Press.

Nathan Curnow is the recent winner of the Josephine Ulrick Poetry Prize. His latest book, *The Ghost Poetry Project*, was named by Cate Kennedy as a 'Best Read' of 2009.

Luke Davies is the author of three novels, four books of poetry, the screenplay *Candy*, the children's book *Magpie* (HarperCollins, 2010), essays and reviews. He has won many awards, including the Judith Wright Award. A fifth volume of poetry, *Interferon Psalms*, is due in 2011.

Bruce Dawe was born in Melbourne in 1930. He joined the RAAF in 1959 and began a teaching career in 1968. He retired from full-time teaching in 1993 and now teaches U3A classes. In 2003, he was awarded a Centenary Medal for distinguished service to the arts through poetry.

Tricia Dearborn is an award-winning Sydney poet and short-story writer. Her first collection was *Frankenstein's Bathtub* (Interactive

Publications, 2001). She was joint winner of the 2008 Poets Union Poetry Prize.

B.R. Dionysius was founding director of the Queensland Poetry Festival. He has two collections of poetry, *Fatherlands* (Five Islands Press, 2000) and *Bacchanalia* (Interactive Press, 2002), and a verse novel, *Universal Andalusia* (soi 3 modern poets, 2006).

Lucy Dougan's most recent book is *White Clay* (Giramondo, 2008). She currently works at UWA in the Westerly Centre.

Laurie Duggan currently lives in England. His most recent books are *Crab & Winkle* (Shearsman, 2009), *The Passenger* (UQP, 2006) and *Compared to What: Selected Poems 1971–2003* (Shearsman, 2005).

Will Eaves is the arts editor of the *Times Literary Supplement*. His novels include *The Oversight* (Picador, 2001), *Nothing To Be Afraid Of* (Picador, 2005) and *The Visitors' Book* (forthcoming 2012). A full collection of poems, *Sound Houses*, is forthcoming in 2011 (Carcanet). He sings with the band Spirit of Play.

Stephen Edgar's most recent book is *History of the Day* (Black Pepper), which was awarded the William Baylebridge Memorial Prize for 2009.

Chris Edwards is the Sydney-based author of *Utensils in a Landscape* (Vagabond, 2001), *A Fluke* (Monogene, 2005) and *Nicked* (Vagabond, 2006). His poems are often collage-based; 'Guileless' borrows phrases from Film D'Ici's 2009 documentary *Marilyn: The Last Sessions*.

Anne Elvey has two chapbooks, *Stolen Heath* (Melbourne Poets Union, 2009) and *Claimed by Country* (PressPress, 2010). She holds honorary positions at Monash University and Melbourne College of Divinity.

Brook Emery has published three books of poetry: *And dug my fingers in the sand* (2000), which won the Judith Wright Award, *Misplaced Heart* (2003) and *Uncommon Light* (2007). All were published by Five Islands Press and shortlisted for the Kenneth Slessor Prize.

Kate Fagan's books of poetry include *The Long Moment* (Salt, 2002), *Thought's Kilometre* (Tolling Elves, 2003) and *Return to a new physics* (Vagabond, 1999). A former editor of *How2*, she is from one of

Australia's pre-eminent folk-music families, The Fagans. Her album *Diamond Wheel* won the NFSA award for Best Folk Album. (www. katefagan.com)

Michael Farrell's most recent books are *A Raiders Guide* (Giramondo, 2008) and *Out of the Box: Contemporary Australian Gay and Lesbian Poets* (co-edited with Jill Jones, Puncher & Wattmann, 2009).

Susan Fealy is a Melbourne writer and clinical psychologist. This year she won the Henry Kendall Poetry Award and was equal second in the Place and Experience Poetry Prize.

Liam Ferney is a Brisbane poet. His first collection is *Popular Mechanics* (Intractive Press, 2004). He has lived in the United States, South Korea and the United Kingdom.

S.J. Finn's poetry has appeared in *Cordite, Snorkel,* Picaro Press and the *Age.* Her novel *This Too Shall Pass* is forthcoming from Sleepers Publishing in 2011.

Lionel Fogarty is a Queensland Murri poet of international acclaim and an Aboriginal rights activist. He has published ten books of poetry and an award-winning children's book. His poetry includes large amounts of Bandjalang dialect and vernacular.

Adam Ford is the author of the poetry collections *The Third Fruit Is a Bird* (Picaro Press, 2008), *Not Quite the Man for the Job* (Little Ark, 1998) and *From My Head* (Adam Ford, 1995). He has written short shories and a novel, and makes zines and comics.

Adam Formosa is a creative-writing student at the University of Wollongong. His work has appeared in *Wet Ink, Voiceworks, dotdotdash* and *Tide.* His poetry lecturers have included Alan Wearne, Bonny Cassidy and Shady Cosgrove.

Angela Gardner won the Arts Queensland Thomas Shapcott Prize in 2006 and has written two collections, *Parts of Speech* (UQP, 2007) and *Views of the Hudson* (Shearsman, 2009). She is the founding editor of the poetry journal *foam:e.*

Claire Gaskin's *A bud* (John Leonard Press, 2006) was shortlisted in the John Bray SA Festival Award. She was the 2009 recipient of the Alan Marshall scholarship.

Jane Gibian is a Sydney poet and librarian whose collections include *Ardent* (Giramondo, 2007) and *Small adjustments and other poems* (*Wagtail* and Picaro Press, 2008).

Keri Glastonbury is a lecturer in creative writing at the University of Newcastle. Her first full-length poetry collection, *Git Salute*, is forthcoming from soi 3 modern poets.

Lisa Gorton's poetry collection *Press Release* (Giramondo, 2007) won the Victorian Premier's Prize for Poetry. She has also written a children's novel, *Cloudland* (Pan Macmillan, 2008).

Robert Gray lives in Sydney. His *Collected Poems* will appear in 2011. His most recent book is a memoir, *The Land I Came Through Last* (Giramondo, 2008).

Martin Harrison's selected poems appear in *Wild Bees* (UWA Press, 2008). He is working on a new poetry collection and a book about reading Australian poetry.

Kevin Hart's most recent books of poetry are *Flame Tree: Selected Poems* (Bloodaxe, 2002) and *Young Rain* (Giramondo, 2008), and *Morning Knowledge* is forthcoming (Notre Dame UP, 2011). He teaches at the University of Virginia.

Matt Hetherington's most recent collection is *I Think We Have* (Small Change Press, 2007).

Barry Hill has won premier's awards for poetry, non-fiction and the essay. His *Necessity: Poems 1996–2006* (Papertiger, 2007) won the ACT's 2008 Judith Wright Award, and his poems have appeared in this anthology since 2004.

Sarah Holland-Batt lives in New York, where she is the W.G. Walker Fulbright Scholar at New York University. Her first book, *Aria* (UQP, 2008), won the Judith Wright Award and the FAW Anne Elder Award.

L.K. Holt's first poetry collection, *Man Wolf Man* (John Leonard Press, 2007) won the 2009 Kenneth Slessor Prize. Her second book is *Patience Mutiny* (John Leonard Press, 2010). She is the publisher of John Leonard Press and editor of *Blast: Poetry & Critical Writing*.

Duncan Hose's first book of poems is *Rathaus* (Inken, 2007). His poems have appeared in *Overland, Cordite, Jacket, Island* and the *Herald Sun*. In 2010 he was the dual runner-up for the Judith Wright Award for New and Emerging Poets.

Lisa Jacobson's verse novel manuscript, *The Sunlit Zone,* was shortlisted for the Victorian Premier's Literary Awards 2009. Her poetry is included in *The Oxford Book of Modern Australian Verse.*

Carol Jenkins's first book of poetry, *Fishing in the Devonian* (Puncher & Wattmann, 2009), was shortlisted in the 2009 Anne Elder and Victorian Premier's Literary Awards

A. Frances Johnson is a writer and painter. She has written a novel about colonial painter Eugene Von Guerard, *Eugene's Falls* (Arcadia, 2007), and a poetry chapbook, *The Pallbearer's Garden* (Whitmore Press, 2008). She teaches at the University of Melbourne.

Jill Jones' most recent book is *Dark Bright Doors* (Wakefield Press, 2010). She is co-editor, with Michael Farrell, of *Out Of the Box: Contemporary Australian Gay and Lesbian Poets.* She lives in Adelaide.

Frank Kellaway has written poems, novels, children's literature and a libretto for George Dreyfus. He is also a painter.

Peter Kenneally is English, a Melburnian of sorts, a poet, reviewer, writer and editor for hire.

Graeme Kinross-Smith is a poet, writer of fiction and photographer. He has much experience in conducting writing workshops and giving readings. His novel *Long Afternoon of the World* (Wakefield Press, 2007) was compared to those of Patrick White and Marcel Proust.

John Kinsella's most recent volume of poetry is *Divine Comedy: Journeys Through a Regional Geography* (UQP, 2008). His *Activist Poetics: Anarchy in the Avon Valley* (ed. Niall Lucy) has just appeared with Liverpool University Press.

Andy Kissane lives in Sydney and has published short stories, a novel and three books of poetry. His most recent collection is *Out to Lunch* (Puncher & Wattmann, 2009).

Anna Krien is a writer of journalism, essays, fiction and poetry. Her poem 'The Last Broadcasters' won the 2008 Val Vallis Poetry Award and her first book is *Into the Woods: The Battle for Tasmania's Forests* (Black Inc., 2010).

Mike Ladd presents *Poetica* each week on ABC Radio National. His most recent book of poems is *Transit* (Five Islands Press, 2007). He experiments with poetry on screen and as audio, and is a member of the poetry performance ensemble Max Mo.

Martin Langford's most recent collection is *The Human Project: New and Selected Poems* (Puncher & Wattmann, 2009). He is the editor of *Harbour City Poems: Sydney in Verse 1788–2008* (Puncher & Wattmann, 2009).

Anthony Lawrence is a poet and novelist. His poems have appeared in numerous Australian and international literary magazines, including *Meanjin, Overland, Poetry Australia, LiNQ, Salt* and *Antipodes.*

Michelle Leber's collection *The Weeping Grass* (Australian Poetry Centre, 2010) places the reader underwater or hovering over river valleys with odd creatures and snappish birds. She is working on a verse novel about the Yellow Emperor of China.

Geoffrey Lehmann had joint custody of three small children in the 1970s and '80s. The hero of his poem is a pale-green Kombivan BLK 258, now deceased.

Kate Lilley's *Versary* (Salt, 2002) won the Grace Leven Prize and was shortlisted for the NSW Premier's Awards. Her second collection, *Ladylike*, is forthcoming from Salt.

Debbie Lim's poems have appeared in many anthologies. She is editorial assistant at *Mascara Literary Review*. In 2009, she won the Rosemary Dobson Prize.

Astrid Lorange is a PhD candidate at the University of Technology, Sydney. She is currently a visiting scholar at the University of Pennsylvania. She writes on Gertrude Stein and is working on a chapbook.

Cameron Lowe has served as editor of the *Ardent Sun* and co-editor of the Geelong-based poetry magazine *Core*. He has published frequently in *Meanjin*, *Southerly*, the *Age* and other periodicals.

Roberta Lowing's poetry has appeared in *Blue Dog* and *Overland*. Her first novel is *Notorious* (Allen & Unwin, 2010). Her first collection of poetry is *Ruin* (Interactive Press, 2010).

Anthony Lynch is a writer, editor and publisher. A collection of his poems is forthcoming from Clouds of Magellan.

Jennifer Maiden was born in Penrith, NSW in 1949. She has won many awards, inlcuding the Christopher Brennan Award for Lifetime Achievement. Her latest collection, *Pirate Rain* (Giramondo, 2010), won the *Age* Poetry Book of the Year.

Rhyll McMaster has worked as a secretary, a burns-unit nurse and a sheep farmer. She has been poetry editor of the *Canberra Times*, a reviewer for the *Sydney Morning Herald* and the *Australian*, a manuscripts assessor for the National Book Council, and a script assessor for the Film Finance Corporation.

Kate Middleton's first book, *Fire Season* (Giramondo), won the Western Australian Premier's Book Award for poetry in 2009.

Peter Minter is a Sydney poet, editor and publisher. His most recent collection of poetry is *blue grass* (Salt, 2006).

Anne Morgan's poetry is collected in *A Reckless Descent from Eternity* (Ginninderra Press, 2009). She is an established children's writer. Her website is www.annemorgan.com.au.

Derek Motion is a writer from the Riverina region of NSW. He blogs at *typingspace*. Some other 2010 poems appear in *Cordite* and *Overland 200*.

Les Murray's work has been published in ten languages. He has won many literary awards, including the T.S. Eliot Award (1996) and the 1999 Queen's Gold Medal for Poetry, on the recommendation of Ted Hughes.

Nguyen Tien Hoang's poems and essays have been published in Australia and abroad, including a collection, *Beyond Sleep* (1990), and the long poem *Watermark* (2006), a homage to the liberal arts and humanities movement that occurred in Hanoi in 1956.

Jenni Nixon is a Sydney poet and performer. Her published work includes *Café Boogie* (Interactive Press, 2004) and *Agenda!* (Picaro Press, 2009). She was commended the Marion Eldridge Award in 2009.

Ouyang Yu, originally from China, now based in Melbourne, writes fiction, non-fiction, poetry and criticism in both English and Chinese. At 55, he has published 55 books and he translates works into either language. (www.ouyangyu.com.au)

Geoff Page is a Canberra-based poet. His latest books are *Agnostic Skies* (Five Island Press, 2006), *Seriatim* (Salt, 2001) and *60 Classic Australian Poems* (UNSW Press, 2009). He has also recently released a CD, *Coffee with Miles* (River Road Press, 2009).

π.O. was raised in inner-city Melbourne. Occupation: draughtsman. Disposition and history: anarchist. His collection of poems is *Big Numbers* (Collective Effort Press, 2008). He has represented Australia at many international festivals and is editor of the experimental magazine *Unusual Work*.

Claire Potter was born in Perth. In 2006 she was awarded an Australian Young Poets Fellowship. Her first full-length collection is *Swallow* (Five Islands Press, 2010).

Peter Rose is a Melbourne poet, novelist and editor. *Rose Boys* (Allen & Unwin, 2002), a family memoir, won the 2003 National Biography Award. His most recent collection is *Rattus Rattus: New and Selected Poems* (Salt, 2005).

Josephine Rowe's poetry and short fiction have been widely published and broadcast. Her collection of short stories, *How a Moth Becomes a Boat*, was published in 2010 by Hunter Publishers.

Robyn Rowland's fifth book, *Silence and its Tongues* (Five Islands Press, 2006) was shortlisted for the 2007 Judith Wright Award. Her new and selected poems appear in *Seasons of Doubt & Burning* (Five Islands Press, 2010).

Brendan Ryan's third collection of poetry is *A Tight Circle* (Whitmore Press, 2008). His second collection, *A Paddock in his Head* (Five

Islands Press, 2007), was shortlisted for the 2008 ACT Poetry Prize. He lives in Portarlington, Victoria.

Gig Ryan has been the poetry editor at the *Age* since 1998. She has published six collections of poetry and a new selection of poems is due out in 2011.

Jaya Savige is the author of *Latecomers* (UQP, 2005), which won the Kenneth Slessor Prize for Poetry and the Thomas Shapcott Poetry Prize. He is currently a PhD candidate at Cambridge University. His second volume, *Surface to Air*, will be published in 2011.

Thomas Shapcott is retired and living in Melbourne. In 2010 he published a collection of poems (*Parts of Us*, UQP), stories (*Gatherers and Hunters*, Wakefield Press) and a memoir (*A Circle Round My Grandmother*, Papertiger).

Craig Sherborne's first poetry collection is *Bullion* (Penguin, 1995). His acclaimed memoir, *Hoi Polloi* (Black Inc., 2005), was followed by *Muck* (Black Inc., 2007), winner of a Queensland Premier's Prize.

Andrew Slattery's chapbook *Canyon* (Australian Poetry Centre, 2009) was launched at the 2009 Sydney Writers' Festival. Peter Porter called it 'a Joycean script that's precise and poetic and with considerable humour'. His first collection, *The Severant*, won the ACT Poetry Prize for an unpublished manuscript.

Vivian Smith grew up in Tasmania and now lives in Sydney. His most recent volume is *Along the Line* (Salt, 2006) and a CD, *The Other Side Of Things* (River Road Press, 2008).

Peter Steele, a Jesuit priest, was born in Perth but has spent most of his life in Melbourne. His most recent publication is *A Local Habitation: Poems and Homilies* (Newman College, 2010).

James Stuart recently completed a Masters of creative arts on poetry and the materiality of language. He was a 2008 Asialink Literature Resident in Chengdu, China. (www.nongeneric.net)

Maria Takolander's first full-length collection of poems, *Ghostly Subjects* (Salt, 2009), was shortlisted for the Queensland Premier's Literary Awards. She teaches literary studies and creative writing at Deakin University in Geelong.

Hugh Tolhurst's *Rockling King* was published by Black Pepper in 2010 and *Filth and Other Poems* (1997) has been reprinted. *Last Requests* by his band The Certifiables was also released in 2010.

John Tranter has published more than twenty collections of verse, including the multi-award-winning *Urban Myths: 210 Poems* (UQP; Salt, 2006). His latest book is *Starlight: 150 Poems* (UQP, 2010). He is the founding editor of *Jacket* magazine and the APRIL project. (johntranter.com)

Mark Tredinnick, winner of the Blake and Newcastle prizes, is the author of eight books, including *The Blue Plateau* (UQP, 2009). His first book of poems is *Fire Diary* (Puncher & Wattmann, 2010).

Petra White's poetry books are *The Incoming Tide* (2007) and *The Simplified World* (2010), both from John Leonard Press. She works as a public servant.

Louise Wakeling is a poet and teacher. Her most recent collection is *Paragliding in a War Zone* (Puncher & Wattmann, 2008). Her current project is a collection of ecopoetry.

Meredith Wattison's books of poetry are *Psyche's Circus* (Australian Poetry Centre, 1989), *Judith's Do* (Penguin, 1996), *Fishwife* (Five Islands Press, 2001), *The Nihilist Line* (Five Islands Press, 2003), and *Basket of Sunlight* (Puncher & Wattmann, 2007). *Terra bravura* (Puncher & Wattmann) is due in 2011.

Chloe Wilson is a PhD candidate at the University of Melbourne and former poetry editor for *Voiceworks*. Her first collection of poems was *The Mermaid Problem* (Australian Poetry Centre, 2010).

Fiona Wright's poetry has been published in journals and anthologies in Australia, Asia and the United States. Her first collection is forthcoming in 2011.